Totem Magic

Totem Magic

Dance of the Shape-Shifter

Yasmine Galenorn

THE CROSSING PRESS
Berkeley / Toronto

The Crossing Press

A division of Ten Speed Press
P.O. Box 7123
Berkeley, California 94707

1-58091-116-1

Cover design by Rebecca Neimark
Text design by Jeff Brandenburg/image-comp.com

Printed in the United States

Contents

Part Two: Totemic Magic

Dedication:

To Pakhit, Luna, Meerclar, and Tara
You will never read this yourselves,
but you know I love you and understand you,
and I know you love me and understand me.

and

To Ellen Cannon Reed
Dear friend, walk lightly
with Isis.
Blessed Be.

Acknowledgments:

First, to my beloved husband, Samwise, who, as always, was a pillar of strength during the time I first wrote this, and without whom I would feel so adrift.

To Panther, Boa, and Peacock, my own totem spirits, for showing me the path of their strength, transformation, and wisdom.

To my tattooist, Nick Graves, for embodying the ink so magically and vividly on my skin.

To all who have shared your stories with me: salutations and may the magic ever run deep within your souls.

To the Spirits of the Animals . . . may we find the wisdom to stop your destruction, which can only mirror the doom of our own species.

And, as ever always: to Mielikki and Tapio . . . my Lady and Lord, you who are so deep within my soul that your breath is now my breath.

Part One

Animal Totems, Guides, and Guardians

I think I could turn and live with animals,
they are so placid and self-contain'd,
I stand and look at them long and long . . .
not one kneels to another, nor to his kind
that lived thousands of years ago,
not one is respectable, or unhappy
over the whole earth.

—Walt Whitman, "Song of Myself"

Foreword

I begin this journey as I begin most of my books: with my own stories—in this case, my personal connections with animal totems and spirits. As I sit at the keyboard, pondering just what this mystical connection with the animal kingdom signifies in my life, Tara, one of my cats, tries to help me type. She chin-butts my hand, happy-drools on my keyboard, and guilt-trips me into petting her.

Animals are everywhere in my life and always have been so. I can't imagine spending my life without having cats around. That bond has become part of my spirituality, as rooted and entrenched into my being as my connection with the gods.

Humans share this earth with many other species. Like all creatures, we are part of the food chain. Our ancestors shared an ancestor with the apes of today, and no matter how much we progress and develop, we share a commonality with all beings that live on the face of this planet. We spring from the earth, and to the earth, we return.

Isn't it time we quit denying that, in the scope of evolution and the time frame of the world, we're a mere step away from the trees we once inhabited? Isn't it time we explore our spiritual connections to the animal kingdom? By forging a spiritual bond with our totem spirits and animal guardians, we discover their powers within ourselves, and in turn, we discover the humanity that exists within them. We forge common bonds. With that connection, perhaps we will at last be able to help others understand why we must prevent the extinction of the vast numbers of endangered species, as well as the destruction of their habitats.

Exploring the world of animal totems and guardians opens up a whole new vista in our spiritual journeys, a vista as rich and varied as is the animal kingdom itself. Through this exploration, we can learn how to strengthen our talents and understand our weaknesses as we follow a shamanic path based on nurturing our connection to the natural world. Diving into the Otherworld, our journeys take us outside of time, into the void where all things meet. When we return, we're transformed and strengthened.

While there are a number of very good "totem magic" books out there, *Totem Magic: Dance of the Shape-Shifter* differs from most of them. Rather than simply giving you lists of animals and the energies they represent, I choose to lead via intuition rather than intellect. After I lay down a foundation for work with these magical energies, I offer you guidelines and ideas for spell work for use with your animal spirits.

Consider me a magical guide on a mystical safari, rather than an expert standing at a podium, presenting a lecture.

This book is for those who have a basic grounding in Witchcraft. In *Embracing the Moon,* I laid the groundwork for what I hoped would become a series of advanced magical books based on the experiential shamanic Witchcraft that I practice. *Totem Magic* is the first of those books.

So join me on an exciting journey into the Otherworld, as we go in search of our connection to the spirits of the animal world.

Blessed Be and Journey Safely,

—the Painted Panther
Yasmine Galenorn

Note: If you want to contact me about this or any of my books, you may write to me via my publishers or reach me through my website, Galenorn En/Visions, at www.galenorn.com.

That inescapable animal walks with me.
Has followed me since the black womb held . . .

—Delmore Schwartz, "The Heavy Bear Who Goes with Me"

Panther Rising:
A Dream of the Jungle

A Vision of the Dream

1991—January

A glimpse of myself in the mirror. I greet my reflection. Don't flinch. Stand straight. Breathe deep, so deep that it feels as if I am saturating my lungs with oxygen. Candles rest on either side of the mirror, and the lights are off. The scent of rose petals from the fresh flowers in the other room drifts in on the gentle currents. Music echoes in surround sound. I have the volume turned so high that the candle flames flicker with the beat.

Freeze frame—strobe effects from flickering wicks heighten my awareness. I am here, focused only on my existence.

Flash—I begin to lose myself in the mirror.

Flash—the room ripples, waves of energy rise.

Flash—the pulse of the drum resounds in my chest.

Flash—my face vanishes and I see a man, Mongol—I know he who he is, with those dark eyes staring back at me. He is me and I am him. We have met this way before.

Flash—my own face returns.

Flash—go deeper into the music, let it suck me down, let the beat overwhelm me.

Flash—the thunder of jungle drums.

Flash—another transformation. Black panther stares at me from the mirror . . . leopard, jaguar, spirit of the big cat. Panther prowling, predators abound. I feel her bloodlust in my heart. Caged within wooden walls, I want to pace, to run under the moon, to prowl. Her eyes are my eyes. Her breath is my breath. She gazes at me from beyond the veil. I open myself, open my heart, open the very spark that makes me who I am, and I find her there. We are one.

Flash—and I am floating through that ethereal haze that exists between the worlds, and then—

Flash—I am back. And she's back, deep inside me, waiting.

Ritual

1991—February

I'm performing a ritual for Bast, the Egyptian Cat Goddess. Panther watches from within my heart, eyes gleaming, head cocked to the side. As always, music swirls around me, a backdrop to trance, an ecstatic escalator to heightened awareness.

My cats gather around, rubbing my legs. A plate of raw steak sits on the altar along with amber and lotus, frankincense and mead. I invoke the Mistress of Cat-Kind and call her name loudly. My Russian Blue begins to purr and taps me with her paw. I invoke Panther and feel the great cat rise within. The steak sits, bloody and terribly fresh. I wince at the thought, but I know that this must be a part of the ritual. Sometimes we have no choice in the playground of the gods.

I lift a piece of the meat and put it in my mouth, waiting for the gorge to rise. Instead, I feel the brilliant taste of blood slide down my throat and the sweetness of the meat on my tongue. A wave of bloodlust races through me, and I begin to devour the meat, dropping tidbits for the cats who are in an ecstatic frenzy; the energy has swept down and caught them up. My conscious mind steps aside as intuition creeps in and I find that I'm hungry, as I have never been before, craving the protein, ripping at the meat with my teeth, letting the music carry me on. The cats are in that belly-rubbing, tummy-tickling, chin-butting orgy of gods-know-what that makes them roll over on their backs and squirm around, legs pawing the air, eyes fastened on me.

When the ritual is over, I look at myself in the mirror and wonder whether I'm possibly going insane. Panther rises a little more every day, and I wonder just how far into this fantasy/dream/memory I can go without losing who I am today. But I have no choice: this is a path down which I must walk, no matter where it leads me. I only hope that I find my way out the other side. If there is another side.

Tattoo

1998—Beltane (May 1)

Today I got my first tattoo. It's nighttime now, and my black panther spirit rests upon my left breast, with a coiling green boa around the forepaws, a peacock feather fan in the back with a pentacle woven into it, foxglove trailing up my shoulder near the tail of the panther, and a fly agaric at the base of the flowers. I'm exhausted, in no small amount of pain, and a little freaked-out. A friend warned me this would happen, that inevitable moment when you look at the fresh tattoo and say, "What the hell did I just do to myself?"

The tattoo is large, and the energy of Panther is there, out for the world to see, for me to wear for the rest of my life. She's no longer trapped inside, hiding. Her time has come, and she and I have merged with a finality that will last through this lifetime. For years, I've known this day would arrive, waited for it with eager anticipation. Now I'm a little bit scared. She peeks through my eyes. As my chest rises and falls, my breath is her breath. I try to rest, try not to touch the raw skin. I look at myself more closely, hold a mirror up to my breast. The artwork is incredibly lush and beautiful. I remember how much I've wanted this, how Panther has been pestering me for years to get her tattooed on my body, and I begin to calm down.

And then, so many years after I first encountered her in my life, I hear her voice. A whisper, really. A low growl. She tells me her name and suddenly she's no longer simply an aspect of the Spirit of the Panther, she's real and breathing, and she's part of me. And so, her name becomes one of my names.

Dream

1998—September

A dream.

I am riding on a bus with a group of people. I know some of them; others I don't. An old woman sits in the back, carrying a skull. She looks at me and says, "Skulda, you must remember Skulda." I don't know who she's talking about. The woman looks to be of African descent. She smiles softly and I turn away. When I look back, she has disappeared.

We drive up a mountain road where the landscape is barren, with sagebrush surrounding us and dark earth, and the night sky reels with stars overhead. When we reach the top of the road, we are overlooking what appears to be an ancient caldera, and within the caldera I see a statue of a giant black panther sitting to one side and a crackling bonfire in the center. Made of black onyx (somehow, in dreams we always know these little details), the statue stands almost one hundred feet tall. People pile out of the bus and spill into the crater. I follow, slowly, feeling a pull that I've never before felt. Magnetic, this force can't be denied.

The people who were with me on the bus begin to dance, drums pound from the distance, and I circle the edges, wary, keeping one eye on the statue. Shadows twist and writhe against the sides of the crater.

And then, I am changing. Transforming. My body bends forward, lengthens. Muscles pull, sinews stretch. The pain is incredible, yet I'm not afraid. My face begins to lengthen, my ears shift shape. Whiskers force out of my cheeks and nose. Claws rip through my fingers and curve, glistening in the moonlight. The drums thunder a furious pace and I metamorphose. I look up to the statue, and the eyes glisten emerald green. The statue comes to life as I begin to race around the circle, stretching my new, feline body. I raise my gaze to the moon hanging golden and full overhead, and a glorious fury rages within. I'm back, and I'm the me I've always been, but have forgotten through time.

The dancers now dance as the ghosts of my tribe, lost so long ago. Their shouts wake the memory of the dead. A man whispers in my ear: "Your people are scattered. You need to gather your tribe again. You lost them; you were the shaman and you lost them."

And then I'm out of the crater, racing through the night, prowling in the treetops, snuffling in the leaves, hunting. I embrace my strength, my freedom. I'm seeking my tribe. The night passes as shadows—some flickers of sight, but mostly of energy. A vortex of imagery, a kaleidoscope of passionate hunting.

Toward dawn, I once again find myself in the crater. The ghosts are gone; the people on the bus have vanished. All that remains in front of the statue is a pile of ancient, ivory bones. Skulls and scattered dreams of a time long past. But I remember. And as I shift back into my human body, I begin to cry, mourning for my lost self, mourning for my people.

When I wake, tears are streaming down my cheeks. All that remains are the images and a poem that can only hint at what I felt.

PANTHER RISING

An ancient crater, blackened lava bed,
dancing moonstruck figures weave roundabout
drumbeats resound, the hearts of those long dead
brought to life by feral passionate shouts.
Onyx statue rises before devout
worshippers, those ancestors I call my own.
Panther rising, emerald gaze shines out
shifting shape, transforming, I am alone.
Into mounds of yellowed ivory bones
others vanish. I prowl beneath the moon
to creep, to sleep, to hunt, to run, to roam.
Swiftly over, my dream recedes too soon.
I waken tense, and listen for the drums
and mourn the loss until the daylight comes.

Who was Skulda? And who were my people? What happened to our tribe? Mysteries, all. Mysteries still.

Looking Back

When I look back, I realize that Panther has always been with me. Even when I was little, there was a big feral black cat connected with my dreams and imagination. I never gave it much thought until my late twenties, when I began to look into the nature of totem magic and animal spirits that guide us, that are part of us. Many people, myself included, seem to have several guardians (or you might call them helpers, guides, or totems), but usually we have a primary one with which we connect on a soul level. The black panther—or black leopard or jaguar if you will—is my primary totem. I have two others: a snake, the green tree boa, and the peacock (not the peahen).

While Peacock has been ethereal—showing up in my dress, my vanity, and my ability to reduce a person to tears with words when I'm in a shrill and irritable mood—he has not appeared in my dreams. He has, however, been with me since I was young. Shortly before I got my peacock tattoo, I discovered a connection between the bird and the Hindu goddess Sarasvati, who rules over language and poetry. As an author, this connection makes perfect sense to me. I am always aware of Peacock's energy when I write, when I dress, and when I present myself to the public. Peacock straightens my posture, lifts my chin, keeps my gaze even. Peacock helps me put my best foot forward, and he also helps me stand up for my rights when I've been taken advantage of. Peacock helps me find the right words at the right time.

Snake, on the other hand, defined herself as a green tree boa around 1990, though she has been with me since I was young, in a generalized "snaky" way. She's come into my dreams upon occasion, however, and in most telling ways.

One night, in 1993—five years before I got my boa tattoo—I was very sick. I had pneumonia and couldn't afford to go to the doctor. That night, I drifted into a light, waking sleep and had this dream:

Mielikki (my patron goddess, the Finnish Goddess of the Hunt) stared down at me as I lay on the bed. A long green boa rose up from the bottom of the bed and slithered into my first chakra. As it did, I blended with its nature and transformed into the snake.

I heard a voice saying, "Eat the poison, eat the poison," and it felt like the snake/me was transmuting all the negative energy in my body. Then I was traveling along the ground and went up over a wall. At the top, the plateau turned into a cliff. A woman wearing flowing orange robes was dancing atop the mesa, and I reared up next to her until I was her height. I looked over the edge and saw a huge statue, carved out of a mountain, hundreds of feet high, of a king cobra.

Then I was back in my bed, still as the snake and yet my own—human—self. It felt like I was trying to go out of body but couldn't quite make it. I called out to a friend. I heard her voice telling me to "unlock your toes" so I reached down, flipped open one toenail, and pressed a button under it.

All of a sudden, my back started splitting open. I was shedding my skin, becoming strong, radiant, and beautiful. I climbed out of my old body, and the skin turned from a snakeskin into the skin of my old self.

Still in the dream, I decided that I needed to perform a ritual to get rid of the old skin, though I kept hearing a voice reminding me to be proud of what my old shell had done for me. I set the skin on a table in the center of the living room, cast a Circle, and called the elements. As I invoked Mielikki and reached out to touch the skin, it burst into flames, then burnt to ashes. When I woke up, I realized I had been doing some heavy-duty transformational magic on the astral level.

The night I got my boa tattoo, I dreamt that I was resting. As I looked over to my right side, Boa slithered off my arm. I was bereft, heartbroken to think that she didn't want to be part of me. I found her in an open-topped aquarium, coiled around a branch. As I reached in, she bit me. Then she slithered back up to coil around my arm again, and I wondered if she was mad at me. When I woke up, I called my friend Andrew, a snake breeder, and he told me that green tree boas are notorious for their quick reactions. They bite at anything that moves because they are arboreal, constantly on the hunt.

This made sense, and I came to peace with the dream. She hadn't bitten me because she didn't want to be part of me; she was simply acting in accordance with her nature, and I was forced to accept that she was a predator above anything else.

At that point, I began to understand that I had been worried about my own predatory (competitive) nature. Unlike a panther, which also has a warm fuzzy side, Snake seems cool and calculating. This aloofness mirrored a part of myself that I've always been afraid might grow too strong. But through working with Boa, I've come to accept that the cool, calculating side of me is extremely helpful. Practical and organized, this aspect of myself ensures that I go about my work in an efficient manner. Boa also keeps me calm during conflicts, and I am able to plan out my strategy without allowing emotion to overwhelm me.

It was at this point that I understood how we can take what seems to be a negative attribute and give it a positive spin.

Each of my totems represents a different aspect of myself. I am part of each animal, linked on a soul level. I discovered my totems early, but not all people connect with them at a young age, and the search isn't always an easy one.

When we begin to delve into the study of animal totems and shape-shifting, the arena can seem overwhelming. *"So-and-so says the bear means this, but Mr. X says it means something else, and I feel close to the bear but neither of those explanations work for me . . ."*

For some, the difficulty rests in never being able to trust their intuition, always feeling uncertain of what the inner self is saying to the conscious mind. *"I think my totem is the wolf, but wolves are popular, so I'm scared I might just be picking an easy totem because everybody else seems to claim it."*

Then there are questions like, *"I think the goose is my totem, but I'm not sure because I had one vision of the goose and nothing more since then,"* and more commonly, *"I really think that I connect with the turtle, but my teacher told me no—she sees a turkey in my aura."*

In Summation

It's no wonder that people get confused. In the coming chapters, we will begin to unravel some of these difficulties and try to smooth out the path to help you discover your animal guides and totems. In the process, I hope to help you develop a closer relationship with the animal kingdom, both within the soul and out in the wild.

If you talk to the animals they will talk with you
and you will know each other.
If you do not talk to them, you will not know them,
and what you do not know, you will fear.
What one fears one destroys.

—Chief Dan George

2

Defining Totem Magic:
A Mystical Safari

The Connection of Animal Spirit to Soul

Just what is a "totem spirit"?

There are many explanations that attempt to define what animal totems are and how we connect to them, and each explanation has value. Just as every teacher brings a different slant with them to the subject they are teaching, so I, too, will offer a unique new perspective on working with totems. Because the metaphysical realm is so vast, and because the universe is, at best, nebulous and ever-changing, I stand by my belief that there can be no one "right" definition or explanation of totems for everybody. There are as many paths to spiritual enlightenment as there are people in the world, and while I firmly believe that we cannot, and must not, ignore science, we must also remember that we have discovered but a fragment of the answers to the world's mysteries.

I have been developing my magical tradition for almost twenty-five years through experiential magic. I've burnt my fingers a number of times; I've seen a number of my spells and invocations work incredible magic, while others failed miserably. From this vantage point, I have come to believe that we can have intrinsic connections with the spirits of the land, the spirits of the Otherworld, and especially the spirits of the animals.

I am not speaking about an intellectual understanding of archetypes, nor am I talking about simply liking animals. I firmly believe that we can do more than just connect on a spiritual level with these spirits. I believe we can actually be a *part* of that animal spirit during the time we exist in human form.

Before I go any farther, let me also add that I'm not talking about the "furry" subculture that has sprung up over the past few years. I make no judgments on the participants, but the furry culture doesn't have anything to do with the magical work I present in this book.

Since everything in the universe is connected, it stands to follow that we have an inherent ability within our essential core to link up with other species, plants, even inorganic material such as rocks and crystals (which I also believe have a form of cellular consciousness) through that universal connection.

We can be part of an animal, part of a plant, part of a place, or part of a rock while still in human form. In the days when magic was still visibly strong in the physical world, shamans from various cultures were able to shape-shift into other forms. I accept that this took place on a physical level. I've played with shape-shifting and have seen what can happen when you blur the edges of "reality" and open the door to other realms.

So when I speak of my totems being a part of me, I do not mean that they are simply a representation of my nature or that they are an animal to which I feel closely aligned. I firmly believe that my soul is part panther, part boa, and part peacock, along with being part human. All of these aspects make up "Yasmine Galenorn."

What about That Word: "Totem"?

Let me address a common concern. There has been a great deal of controversy over the co-opting of aboriginal traditions. I have strong opinions on the subject that I may address in a future book, but for our purpose here, let me say this: Almost all cultures have had mystical connections with animals as part of their heritage. The Finns, Celts, Norse, Maori, Native Americans, Aztecs, you name it—all of these cultures had special affiliations with animal spirits in one way or another. This is a worldwide phenomenon, and no one tribe, culture, or region of the world can lay sole claim to the practice.

There are several words and phrases that we can use to describe our connection with animals and animal spirits. "Totem" is the word most commonly used, and perhaps this is where the source of the controversy rests since the origin of that word is attributed to the Ojibwa word *nintotem*. The *American Heritage Dictionary* defines a totem as "an animal, plant or natural object serving among certain primitive peoples as the emblem of a clan or family by virtue of an asserted ancestral relationship."

Then we have totemism, which the same dictionary defines as "the belief in kinship through common totemic affiliation or the identification of an individual or group with a totem."

In a sense, if we take this literally, a totem is not an animal spirit connected with our soul so much as a symbol of our nature. However, it has come to stand for, in modern metaphysical circles, a different sort of connection, namely that of a soul link with an animal spirit who represents a part of our nature, and with whom we have a mystical connection in the physical world.

Animal Spirit Totems and Shape-Shifting

There are a number of different ways in which we may communicate with animal spirits. When we find that our connection with a particular animal spirit goes deeper than just having them serve as a guide in our life, we can call this our "animal spirit totem," or more simply, our "totem." This link is forged deep within our soul on the astral or shamanistic level. And only the individual can truly determine when this link is present. This bond generally won't dissipate and lasts throughout our lifetime from when we first meet the spirit.

We may have known our animal spirit totem since birth, or we may develop a growing awareness of the spiritual connection as time progresses. This varies per individual and for some will not appear until it's time for us to begin working with our animal spirit. This often takes place after we've reached a certain level in our spiritual journey.

This connection between animal spirit and human is a very intimate experience. The magic of reaching out and sensing that primal, feral part of the self is unlike any other journey of self-discovery. We are all part animal; we evolved from ancestors who lived hand to mouth, who knew nothing of the mechanics of the world around them. When we first looked to the skies and wondered, "Are we more than this?" we began our path out of a life based solely on survival instincts. But deep in our psyche, our race memory still remembers being deeply involved with the natural realm during a time before thought and intellect created the division that now stands between ourselves and nature.

While we can never go back, we can still touch upon that sense of the primal, that sense of being an intricate part of the natural cycle, sans modern world, sans human nature.

When we reach for this bonding with the animal spirits, we reach past ethics, we reach past belief systems, and we tune directly into our primal roots. In this state, we view the world as a swirling, kaleidoscopic realm of experience; we leave conscious thought behind and work on a subconscious level. We invite the wild woman or wild man out of hiding, only when we do so in this context, wild woman/man becomes a *chimera*—a being with two distinctly different genetic parents—taking on some of the attributes and energies of the animal to which she or he is linked.

When taken to extremes, this exercise leads to what I would call a modern form of shape-shifting. I add the qualifier "modern" because, as far as I know, we've lost the abilities that allowed us to fully assume the shape of the animal in the physical world.

I do believe that the ability to shape-shift existed, that this practice actually took place and on a regular basis. I also believe that we still can go prowling as our totem animal on the astral realm. But in our society, which stresses logic and reason, it's difficult to move past our left-brain conditioning. Not to mention the fact that we have firmly grounded ourselves in a world where magic is relegated to the playroom and big-screen fantasies.

However, just because we can't fully shape-shift into our animal totem on a physical level, doesn't mean we can't learn how to go out on the astral plane and take its form during trance work. Nor does this lack of modern tangible shape-shifting invalidate our connections to the animal spirits. By working with animal spirits, we can incorporate their energies and abilities into our lives in ways that are beneficial to us as human beings, and in this way strengthen ourselves in our mundane lives while increasing our bond to our totem spirit and symbol. '

Shape-shifting on the spiritual level can be exhausting when we first seek to master this practice. When I first encountered the discipline, I stumbled onto it by accident. I briefly discussed this in *Embracing the Moon,* but I will go into it in more depth now.

There was a point in time back in 1990–1991 when my panther totem decided it was time to come to the surface. I began to dream of her on a regular basis. When I walked down the street, she walked beside me. I could feel her breath on my left hand, for she runs by my left side. It seemed that everywhere I looked, I'd find pictures, articles, and shows involving black panthers. She appeared in my guided journeys, she took over my visions, and it was at this time that I knew I would someday have to wear her on my body as a tattoo in order to seal the connection.

As I said before, I've always known Panther walked beside me and inside me. But the time came when I had to unlock the cage within me in which I kept her. Big cats cannot be domesticated, cannot be tamed. We can only coexist with them on their terms. She wanted to be a strong part of my life as the soul partner she is, and if I didn't let her out of confinement, she would turn on me and I'd begin to self-destruct.

It was out of her desire to emerge more fully that I began a series of rituals, meditations, and trance workings intended to open the doors that kept her pushed down deep inside of me rather than only letting her stare out through my eyes.

At first these rituals were mainly meditations, a study of what panthers were like, getting to know them on a mundane level. Gradually they became deeper, more experiential, more physical and less cerebral. A dinner, feasting on raw steak to understand the bloodlust cravings of cats set off a frenzy among my own cats—a joyful and almost orgiastic ritual of purring and rolling around in front of my altar. I realized that the energy I was conducting was tangible to others besides myself.

I began to work with sessions of visionary trance work, using the mirror to watch my face shift and change in the candlelight. Back I went . . . back past lives that flickered across my face like the leaves of a book. Then I came to my Mongolian self. He was a warrior—and he was a part of my past. Proud, tall, meeting my gaze across the years, something within him recognized my search for Panther, and so we connected across the sands that make up the passing of the eons within the Dreamtime world, where there is no division—where we can reconnect with our other selves that have gone on before.

And then again, moving backward to faces who had no name, to beings who lived in the world before civilization domesticated our race. There I met myself as Panther. Woman, panther, panther-woman. Shape-shifter in some ancient tribe of jaguar people. She held no high titles, no honors and cheers. She simply lived in two worlds at once, living in the Dreamtime during an age when magic walked hand in hand with daily life. And then farther back. Back to the core— back to the primal essence of my panther spirit, before that aspect of my soul entered the human realm. And there was the beginning of my connection with the Spirit of the Panther. And there she was, waiting for me to find my way back to her.

After I became adept at watching my face change in the mirror, at not fearing the shifting of spirits across my own countenance, I began to call Panther up from those depths. I invoked her spirit in my meditations; I sought her in my ritual. One night she rose within me, and I looked over at the woman who was my girlfriend at the time. She stared at me, and I knew she was seeing the superimposition of spirit upon spirit. She had been working with her own totems, and as I paved the way for Panther to emerge, so she worked with her own—Fox gleamed out of her eyes, smiled behind a feral cunning grin. We would spend evenings in trance work, ecstatically dancing our totems out of the shadows, invoking them into our daily lives, watching mist rise in the room as we took our shape-shifting as far as we dared (as far as we could?).

We let our totems speak through us. We channeled their energy and listened to their guidance. Willing to take risks in order to explore these animalistic sides of ourselves, we slid into trance on a nightly basis, working with improvised and spontaneous rituals as we delved into the shadow work of the gods. We employed shamanistic Witchcraft—experiential, grounded in experience and primal energies—rather than rote rituals and memorized scripts. We ran with the gods that summer.

And then, as suddenly as it had come, the intensity slipped away. We found ourselves on the edge of chaotic burnout and went our separate ways. But what I learned would stay with me in a way that little else has. The connection to my primal totemic self led the way into other realms, led the way for me to integrate Panther into my daily life.

Around this time, Green Boa began to rise up, and Peacock, and though they never have been as strong or as in-my-face as Panther, they are solidly there, foundations on which my being rests. I knew that in time I would bear their images on my body, along with Panther's. I didn't know when, but the visions of where they would be placed, of how they would look, firmly took hold, and I kept them in my heart, waiting for the day when it would be the right time to get the tattoos.

In 1998 my second book had just come out and I sat there, holding my first royalty check, thinking, "It's time for my tattoos." So I began the journey toward having my totems tattooed on my body. Bringing their images forth on my body had far-reaching effects. Not only did this strengthen my bond to my animal spirits, it also created a powerful sense of armor with which to shield myself from negativity. I was empowered in a way that I had never before felt.

And now? Panther is always walking in my footsteps; she dances with me in the dance that is my life; she breathes the breath of my existence. When I look up, she looks through my eyes. When she examines an image, I see through her gaze. When I reach out, Boa guides my arm. When I walk, Peacock shifts my posture and stance.

What Are We Seeking from Totem Magic?

What are we are seeking from totem magic? The answer depends entirely on the individual. The benefits of working with totem magic are many. The discovery of our totems can offer us a solid sense of communion with the natural kingdom. We create a bond with the planet and with other species. We lose the sense of alienation we can develop in our attachments to cities and technology. While human inventions have benefited our race in more ways than we can count, they also bring with them the double-edged sword of dividing us from our essential animal natures.

The magical side of totem work takes us into the realm of the mystic, the shaman, the Witch, the visionary. We not only seek to *understand* these animal spirits, we seek to *become one* with them.

Much as the ancient (and some modern) hunters, we slide into trance and let the pounding of drums transport us into a world of swirling energy where, like some universal kaleidoscope, our souls superimpose with those of the animals with which we connect. We dance their dance, let them speak through our bodies, lose ourselves in their nature, and come up swallowing water as we drown under the waves of energy. We die and are reborn in a frenzy of ecstatic rites.

In essence, our journey along this route comes to one common quest: *Through our totems, we seek to define ourselves and join the circle of life.*

The link to a power animal makes it easier to understand ourselves. By studying the strength of the bear, her hibernation cycle, and the protective Mother-energy that she exudes, we then understand our own cycles of retreat, desires to nurture, and personal power. Through meditating on whale song, we grasp the dynamics of language and storytelling. Each animal is imbued with myriad qualities—both strengths and weaknesses. When we discover our soul's connection to one animal in particular, we can be on the lookout for those same attributes within ourselves and thereby work through what we perceive as faults, while strengthening what we see as our advantages.

These animal spirits take us on journeys into the hidden depths of our subconscious, into the Otherworld, the Underworld, and the realm of the gods.

They help us transform, change, and shift our energies. Our totems, however, are far from simple messengers or mounts that other animal spirit guides might be. For our totems are with us for the long haul; they weave in and out of our lives in a complete and intimate manner.

Animal Guides and Guardians

An *animal guide* (be it in flesh or in spirit only) will sometimes come to our aid when we need its particular energy and then leave when we no longer need that aid. Sometimes they are the spirit of what we usually think of as a mythological beast, and they often show up in our dreams before manifesting in our daily lives.

There was a period when my black panther was joined by a spotted leopard. Panther walked on my left side, Leopard on my right. Leopard seemed to be there to balance out Panther's shadow side. Eventually, when I found balance in my life, Leopard vanished.

Often we encounter an animal guide in our guided meditations and visualizations. They enable us; they empower us during the current phase of our life lessons. Or we might find that we haven't been paying attention to omens or recurring themes in our lives, and an animal guide may show up to lead us back to the path or to teach us how to listen.

If, for example, we've ignored the signs that we need to take a more active leadership role at work, we might find Mountain Lion showing up in our dreams to remind us of the need to accept our role as a leader or teacher. Mountain Lion walks alone and does not follow; we can't assume a sheepish mindset while running the energy of Puma. Perhaps sometime in the future we'll need to take a backseat again, and then another animal, less assuming and more oriented toward teamwork, will enter our journey.

An *animal guardian* usually appears for the express purpose of protection or warning—such as the polar bear I encountered after I broke up with my ex. I'm convinced the guardian took this form because I was, at the time, heavily relying on comfort from the stuffed polar bear that sat on my bed. I would talk to Frosty, cry on his belly, hug him when I was scared and lonely, and before long, I noticed that there was a polar bear roaming the apartment (in the astral realm, of course), keeping watch over me. This comforted me far more than I can ever give thanks for, and when I finally grew used to being alone again and my fear faded, the guardian spirit quietly faded away.

At times, an animal guide or guardian may manifest into our lives on a physical level—as our totems occasionally will do. For the most part, however, our work with these spirits will be on the astral level. If we do encounter them in the flesh, it may be through the sighting of a hawk, an elk, or another wild beast. Or perhaps we find that a dog or cat has attached themselves to us, and they stay with us through some difficult period in our life and then move on. Their departure can be traumatic if we've become attached to them, but sometimes trauma goes hand in hand with growth, and we have to learn to accept these comings and goings with the realization that, during our life, we will lose people and animals. It's never easy, but it's part of the natural cycle.

Messengers of the Gods

In most shamanistic cultures, animal spirits are also considered messengers of the gods. The King Stag represented the elemental spirit of the Hunter and was considered a sign of royalty for many. His appearance often signified a change coming to the kingship of the land.

Whales and dolphins bring messages from the ancestors. Some traditions consider whale song to be a history of the past, back beyond human recollection. Seals are magical creatures, embodying the faeries called Selkies, who slip in between the worlds to interact with our kind.

Birds have long been thought to be harbingers of divine communication, bringing the words of the gods to earth. When we think about it, this makes a lot of sense. Birds can fly, an ability that—until modern science—has been looked upon as supernatural. We see them descend from parts unknown to land in trees, on our roofs, on the ground at our feet. They screech out their warnings;

some birds even pick up our own language and "talk" to us. Then they take wing again and fly out of our lives, heading into the sky toward the heavens.

So it seems natural that birds carry with them divine messages, that their appearance foretells the future and brings advice from the realms of the faerie, the deities, and the spirits. In fact, birds are so connected with the world of invisible and unseen forces that Mongolian shamans believe that the cuckoo bird represents the shaman and shamanic powers. Cloth cuckoo birds are commonly fastened on the shoulders of the shaman's costume. Killing the bird is definitely taboo.

Daniela, my blood-oath sister, has Cougar for her main totem, but a few years ago Raven started making an appearance in her life, and she knows it has something to do with her connections to the Norse path. Daniela has been a Priestess of Freyja since 1992 and works extensively with Odin.

When she moved to Berlin, Germany, Daniela started feeling the energy of the northern traditions more. She said, "The latest and most profound event happened recently. I had decided to treat myself to lunch. The restaurant had just opened, so the only people there were the waiter, the cook, and the bartender. As I walked in the door, which was propped open, and said hello, one of them pointed to a spot next to me and asked, 'Is that your bird?' I looked down and, sure enough, a large black raven was standing by my side. Needless to say, I was startled and blurted out, 'I've never seen that bird before in my life!' I wasn't quite sure what to do, so I walked to the farthest corner of the restaurant and sat down. The raven hopped up on the nearest table and began jumping from tabletop to tabletop until he was next to me. I asked him, 'Are you Hugin or Munin?' [Odin's mystical ravens, Thought and Memory] The raven cawed once and flew out the door. I truly wish I spoke bird, since I still am not sure what the answer was."

For Daniela, the raven signified a message from Odin.

Sometimes the messages we receive involve transcendence of a sort. According to legends, Thunderbirds—a Native American winged creature—carry prayers to the Great Spirit and bring messages to Earth from the gods. Thunderbirds rule over thunderstorms. To be struck by Thunderbird's lightning either brings enlightenment or destruction. There are a variety of stories about the origin of the Thunderbird. Some claim he is a magical being of both malign and benevolent natures who comes from the Great Spirit. Others believe Thunderbirds are actual huge birds of prey who prefer humans for their food.

Summoning Animal Guides and Guardians

We can summon a guardian animal to work with us, be it the spirit of an animal or a mythological creature. While we can invoke these spirits as thought forms for guardians or for other aid should we need it, we must always be very respectful of them and be very cautious when calling them. They are not under our command, nor should we attempt to control or take power over these beings.

Invoking another entity in an attempt to control it for your own purposes is an act akin to controlling someone through fear on the physical level, and it's wrong, plain and simple. If you're considering summoning up a creature who *must* be controlled due to the havoc it could wreak, then you'd better take another look at your ethics.

However, when you properly invoke a thought form or spirit for protection, be prepared, because they might move right in and make your home their home. A few years back, Samwise and I summoned the spirit of an ancient elk to walk the halls of our home. I'd been gifted with an elk skull. It's weathered so the bone has taken on a sheen the color of the moss that was growing on it, and the tines have been worn away.

The elk was obviously a large one and old; a winter kill, it probably died of starvation, and the skull had been sitting in the crotch of an oak tree for a number of years. I set it aside for several months until I could envision what I was supposed to do with it. I have to admit that I find it funny when someone new to our home walks into the dining room, sees a lovely table set with crystal dishes and china and teacups, and then spots the various skulls and bones around the house. Sometimes eclecticism can be a little disconcerting.

One day as I was sitting at the table reading my *Victoria* magazine, I had a flash of vision. I could see the skull perched atop the shelving that runs near our fireplace, and the skull was to be the home of a guardian spirit. I prepared the bone for hosting a spirit by cleansing and smudging it, warding it against anything negative, then tucked a packet of herbs inside the back and used a mixture of brown and green watercolors, diluted very thin, to even out the mottled, mossy patina.

After the skull was prepared, I told Samwise we needed to do a ritual of invocation. Tapio (my patron god—the Finnish God of the Forest) was guiding me on this; his presence was subtly yet undeniably present through the whole process. After casting a Circle and invoking the elements and then Tapio and Mielikki, I began to summon the guardian spirit. I could feel Tapio opening the gateway, and just then this huge, ancient, deep-forest-dwelling elk spirit walked into our living room. I could see the spirit as a shimmering field of energy. Right then Samwise spoke up and said, "It's here, I can see it." He then proceeded to describe the same vision I was having, and at that point the spirit slid into the skull.

Now you have to understand this: Samwise is Pagan, but he isn't a Witch. By his own admission, he doesn't tend to be extraordinarily alert on a psychic level. So I have to confess that when he told me what he was sensing, my first thought was, "If Sam can see this spirit, then it's *really big!*"

After the spirit had entered the skull, I asked it if it had a name it wanted to be identified by. I heard the word "Krikki" (pronounced Kry-ky). Later, I looked it up on the Net and, though I couldn't find a direct translation, it did indeed seem to be a Finnish name.

So we have a Finnish deep-woods elk spirit running around our house, and every time there's some weird glitch of energy, I sense him lumbering through the hall to check it out. When asked what offerings he would like to help "fuel" his energy, he asked for apples, salt, and leaves. Ever since he came to live with us, we've kept a basket of apples near the fireplace for him, and we change them once a week. If we wait too long, he gives us a nudge, and when we finally change the apples, we can physically feel him eating their essence. I don't know how long he'll be content to stay—he is free to come and go as he will. He's ended up being a long-term resident in our home, and he is welcome to make his home with us the rest of our lives.

Spirit of the (Fill in the Blank)

When I say something like "the Spirit of the Wolf," I'm speaking not of an individual animal spirit, but of the overall spirit of all wolves—the supreme spiritual pool of wolf energy, so to speak.

The Spirit of the Wolf, for example, speaks through many deities, through many cultures and lands. It can be found wherever wolves walk or once walked. The same is true with the other animals, birds, and so forth. When we have dreams with animal spirits in them, if the animal doesn't seem to be a distinct individual but is instead a representative of the species, then we have been visited by the spirit of that species.

Usually, when we touch upon these essential spirits or energies, we have something to learn from the species in general, rather than being led or guided by an individual member. This means that we are most likely lacking in a quality or attribute inherent within the nature of that species, or that we are being given an answer to some problem we've been having through their example. If we begin to dream of a pride of lionesses, perhaps we need to work on our teamwork skills. If we encounter flock after flock of ravens, then perhaps we are not attending to our magical practices enough. Have a rash of spider sightings in your house? Perhaps your communications have been garbled or you are weaving yourself into a web of lies and half-truths.

Of course, if you don't know what your totems are, there is the chance that they are asserting themselves and trying to get your notice. You will have to ascertain that for yourself, and there are a number of rituals and exercises that you can use for this work.

Familiars

Familiars are animals we live with who choose to be partners in our magical rites; you might call them soul mates of an animal nature. Since working with familiars is a subject in itself, we will save that for another book.

In Summation

Totem magic takes many forms, and there are rituals from cultures all over the world that are meant to aid the seeker of such knowledge. When we start on this journey, it can be a little frightening. After all, we are interacting with actual spirits here—spirits of animals and energy beings. We are delving into a realm that our Westernized society scoffs at as primitive, belonging only to "savages." Of course, with our culture's current politically correct consciousness, people are quick to give lip service to the traditional beliefs of Native Americans and other aborigines, but I still believe it's only lip service for most of the populace, rather than acceptance that these are legitimate and powerful beliefs.

So it can be difficult for some people to approach totem work when they've been taught to view life through a series of academic filters. They come from a scholarly point of view seeking archetypes, expecting metaphor, and instead find *very real* energies, spirits, and beings with which they must then interact.

When you begin your journey, expect the path to be rocky at times, even a little nerve-racking. As you would respect a venomous snake because it can poison you, so should you respect the Spirit of the Snake—for it composes the energy pool from whence all the snakes' venom comes. And this is true for all the animal spirits.

Once we strip away our egos that insist we, as humans, are more powerful than other beings, we can approach totem animal work with an attitude of respect, curiosity, and wonder. In this manner, we will achieve far more than if we blunder in, demand to be shown our power animals, then complain if they aren't what we hoped for or expected.

To bear he spake these measures:
"Otso, thou my beloved,
Honey-eater of the woodlands,
Let not anger swell thy bosom;
I have not the force to slay thee,
Willingly thy life thou givest
As a sacrifice to Northland.
Thou hast from the tree descended,
Glided from the aspen branches,
Slippery the trunks in autumn,
In the fog-days, smooth the branches.
Golden friend of fen and forest,
In thy fur-robes rich and beauteous,
Pride of woodlands, famous Light-foot,
Leave thy cold and cheerless dwelling,
Leave thy home within the alders,
Leave thy couch among the willows,
Hasten in thy purple stockings,
Hasten from thy walks restricted,
Come among the haunts of heroes,
Join thy friends in Kalevala.
We shall never treat thee evil,
Thou shalt dwell in peace and plenty,
Thou shalt feed on milk and honey . . . "

—*The Kalevala*

Excerpt from Runo XLVI: "Otso the Honey-eater"

Translated by John Martin Crawford, 1888

Calling the Spirits:
Discovering Your Animal Totems

The Journey of Discovery

The journey to uncovering our totems can be a long and sometimes frustrating one. Add to that the fact that our animal spirits are not always what we hoped they would be, and one might wonder, why bother? But there are many benefits to working with totem magic, and even if our totems aren't what we wish they were, they are almost always what we *need* them to be.

Too often, we project our desires onto an image that represents an inner vision of what we wish to be rather than what we are. Or we want to go with the trends and latch onto what is popular at the moment. While all sounding rather exotic, when you look at them, my totems are vicious by human standards. Two predators and a shrill, mean-tempered bird. Yes, I do think they are beautiful, but sometimes I'd like to have a totem with a gentler nature. However, that wouldn't be true to *my* nature.

Also, my totems are not those of my gods. Though I honor and revere the animals that represent my deities and even wear them in my tattoos, I don't connect with them on the same soul level that I do with my own totems.

Each person comes to their totems in a unique and individual way. Starspirit met her red-tailed hawk totem on the physical realm.

"A red-tailed hawk took up residence in the trees next to my garage. I live in a small inner-city lot that has a wooded area behind the house. The hawk was flying through the neighborhood one day, and the boy up the street promptly took out his BB gun and tried to shoot the bird. I grabbed the gun away from the kid, telling him it was a federal offense to shoot a bird of prey in the state of Ohio. The hawk landed on the telephone pole in front of my house. Well, I just looked up at the hawk and said, 'It would be very nice of you to let me have one of your feathers.' The hawk looked down at me, pulled out a small feather from his breast and let it fall to the ground by my feet. My husband is Native American, and it's an honor to receive a feather, so we sprinkled cornmeal around the area in which the feather fell along with a few chunks of deer meat. The hawk watched as I tied the meat to the bushes, and after we went back into the house, we watched through the window as he had his feast."

In a method similar to the Native American traditions of the vision quest, KG and Ginger met their totem animals through drumming ceremonies and dreams.

Ginger says, "On my first drumming journey to the Underworld in the mid-80s, I met a mountain lioness. Over the years, and even quite recently, people have seen a 'large cat lounging in a tree' around me, so I think it is perhaps a permanent animal spirit guide. I dance with it quite often, especially when I am in a crowd of people, or when I am in a meeting at work. I am extremely comfortable with its properties of solitude, confidence, and survival."

KG's visions helped lead them to the land on which they settled and brought them to the skull of the elk totem that guards the permanent Circle in their grove.

Ginger continues, "KG's first drumming journey was quite spectacular. He rode a large elk up 'The World Tree' and met a little old man who was gardening in the clouds. KG asked the man for a little prosperity to come into our lives. A few days later, my mother called. We owned some property in Oklahoma and had been leasing it for a long time for very little money. A man who lived next to the property came out of his house one morning and, in our field, he saw the largest buck he had ever seen. It stared at him, and for some reason, that sighting spurred him on to find out who owned the property. He contacted my mother, and we ended up putting the property on the market, and so we made the money to buy the property we now own. When we bought our mobile home, the owners gave us the huge Wapato elk skull that we keep on our north altar."

So our totem animal spirits manifest in many ways—from a physical encounter to a shamanistic visionary experience. Each manifestation, each meeting, is valid, and in the end, it doesn't matter whether we meet an elk by the side of the road or dream of it. What does matter is that we listen to our inner guidance and pay attention to the signs and symbols that are trying to help us along our spiritual paths.

When we first set out in search of our totems, we should understand that the journey might take longer than we hope. It's also important to integrate several methods for meeting our totems rather than relying solely on dream work or intuition. Read through the following methods and pick those that sound best for your own circumstances. Don't ignore a particular exercise just because you've never tried it before; for example, if you don't work well with your dreams then try guided meditation instead. Explore, experiment, and create your own synthesis.

Dreaming of Your Totems

When ready to discover our totem animals, we might wish to start by invoking them into our dreams or working with them through lucid dreaming. While it can be very difficult to control our dreams, we can set up the circumstances to encourage our subconscious minds to reveal hidden information while we are in the sleep state. Some people can hone these skills enough to actually direct the course of their dream work.

There are a variety of ways that you can create your own nightly ritual suited to your needs. A personalized ritual is more apt to work for you.

Meditation

Meditate on a nightly basis for fifteen minutes to half an hour before you go to sleep. Do this after you are already in bed, so you don't disrupt the flow of your subconscious mind once you've begun the process.

See yourself walking out of a shadowed forest onto an open plain. The light from the moon shines down to surround you and bathe you in its radiant brilliance. As you walk to the center of the open field, the stars swirl around you, and you begin to spin, like a Sufi dancer, twirling in ecstatic abandonment. See yourself spinning faster and faster, and as you spin, your image begins to blur. A cavalcade of animals surrounds you in the vortex of energy—here a lion, there a bear, over there an elk, flying overhead a hawk. See the shapes flow in and around you. Become part of the tableau; join the many animals in the cosmic dance. Take three deep breaths and call out to them, saying: "During my sleep, come forth, you who are my totem spirits and animal guides. Let me see you, know you, become you."

Then, before they can answer, turn over and go to sleep, letting your mind drift until you do. Don't try to force the images to obey, don't try to create an ending for the meditation; simply let the imagery work on your subconscious. In the morning, before you get out of bed, record whatever dreams or snippets of dreams you can remember and the feelings accompanying these dreams. Continue this for a week or two and see what emerges. Look for recurring images, patterns, animals, encounters, or whatever seems to speak to you as important.

Herbal Tinctures and Concoctions

Several herbal teas and mixtures can magically enhance your psychic explorations. None of the following suggestions are to be used for a medicinal diagnosis, and if you are taking any prescription medication, always get your doctor's approval before adding herbal supplements of any kind.

Mugwort tea is especially good for dream work; use one teaspoon per cup of steaming water (never boil the water for any tea, this will reduce some of the effectiveness of the herbs and will alter the flavor). Drink one cup before bed.

Warning: Do NOT drink mugwort tea if you are pregnant; it could harm your developing child or bring on a miscarriage. You can also use chamomile tea to induce a drowsy sensation before sleeping. Valerian root tea produces a somnolent state. Again, use one teaspoon of tea per cup of steaming-hot water.

Tinctures can be helpful in promoting psychic work of this nature. A tincture is a blend of herbs, spices, and alcohol. Some taste terrible, but they can induce a subtle change on the psyche. One in particular that I've made is especially good for trance work, though I warn you: friends who have tried it have labeled the flavor as "electric mold." One good friend provided the name, Divine Outfreakage Tincture. I personally think that once you get used to the pungent nature, it's rather comforting.

DIVINE OUTFREAKAGE TINCTURE

> 4 cups vodka
> $1/2$ cup honey
> 1 cup mugwort
> $1/2$ cup kava kava
> $1/2$ cup galangal root
> 1 tablespoon ground cinnamon
> $1/4$ cup valerian root
> 12 cloves

Heat the vodka in a nonmetallic pan but *do not boil.* Add the honey and stir to blend. Add the herbs and simmer over low heat for twenty minutes. Cool and pour into large jar; cover and place in dark cupboard. (Do not strain.)

Twice a day for twenty-one days, take the jar out and shake the contents. If the herbs have absorbed all the vodka, add more (the herbs *will* expand). At the end of three weeks, strain the contents into a clean jar, cap, and store in the refrigerator. Discard the strained herbs. Drink one-fourth cup before sleeping or meditating. As with all alcoholic beverages, please use this tincture wisely—do not drive after drinking, and keep it out of reach of children.

As far as substitutions, well—this particular mixture is one in which I don't advise substituting. If you don't have the ingredients, then I suggest you use a different concoction.

Working with the Moon's Energies

Power increases during the full moon, and Witches often use this time for culminating rituals and spells. Power during the new moon hides within the psyche, a time when we delve into hidden issues. This is an ideal time for ferreting out information about our totem animals. To do so, procure a piece of obsidian or black onyx (obsidian is very sharp so be careful with it unless it's rounded and polished), a black cloth, a small hand mirror that has been washed with mugwort tea and vinegar water, a white votive candle in an enclosed holder, and a chalice with New Moon Water in it. (See appendix 1 for information on New Moon Water and casting a Circle.)

About half an hour before you go to bed, cast a Circle in your bedroom and lay out a miniature altar. Hang the mirror over your bed so it's facing the foot, and cover it with the black cloth. Set the candle on your dresser and light it. With the chalice nearby, quiet your mind with a simple meditation—don't go into an elaborate guided journey here. Hold the onyx or obsidian, and let your mind fall into a quiet and restful state. When you are ready for bed, raise the chalice and say:

⁓

Let my mind be opened to the mysteries of my animal totems.
Let my conscious mind and my subconscious mind meet.

⁓

Drink the water. Pull the cloth off the mirror and envision energy pouring from the mirror. Say:

⁓

Let this cleansed and protected portal guide me into the Dark Moon
mysteries of my psyche. Let me see what I need to see, as I call upon
those animal spirits with whom I am connected.

⁓

Place the stone on your dresser and blow out the candle. Leave the Circle up and go to sleep. In the morning, jot down notes from any dreams that you had and the feelings surrounding those dreams. This ritual will encourage your subconscious to open up; the mirror is used as a focal point through which energy may travel.

After you wake up and record your dreams, open the Circle and wash the mirror in a mixture of mugwort tea and vinegar water and place it in a safe place.

Drumming in Your Totems

As we saw with KG and Ginger, shamanic drumming can be used to catalyze the search for totem animal spirits. Drumming is an ancient art, known worldwide and used extensively in many religions and cultures as a form of trance inducement and as a hypnotic guidance system. The drums mirror our heartbeats and the pounding sensations of our ecstasy.

One of the first things I learned when I started drumming is that anything can be used for a drum if you don't have a standard instrument. I started practicing on a round wooden tabletop. I also found that a plastic two-liter soda bottle, when filled partway with water, makes a good practice instrument. During some of our get-togethers and drumming circles, my friends and I have used everything from wood blocks and sticks to huge ten-gallon plastic jugs suspended upside down between two trees for drumming. Use your imagination; be sure to look in your kitchen. Pots and pans make good drums and cymbals; two wooden spoons can stand in for drumsticks. Experiment and have fun as you get used to beating out rhythms and patterns.

If you want to buy a drum, you should try out several to get the feel for them. If you like to dance around while drumming, you probably want a lighter drum that is easy to carry or that has a strap so you can wear it. I'd recommend looking into a *bodhran*—a frame drum with a beater (sometimes double-headed)—or a *doumbac,* which can be worn with a sash if made of a lighter material like wood. The ceramic *doumbacs* are better played while sitting. If you choose to drum while standing or sitting in one place, you might also look into congas or other types of standing drums, but these can run into a heavy investment of money, so make sure you truly enjoy drumming before you run out and buy a set. Remember that a skin head will need occasional tightening while a plastic or synthetic head will generally stay tight.

If you can't drum for some reason, or prefer not to, you might consider using a tambourine, a rattle, or a string of bells. These are excellent percussive instruments.

Once you have gotten the feel for the beat, and it doesn't take all that long to learn simple patterns unless you are rhythmically challenged, you can begin working with your drum in trance. I've found that it generally makes no difference to me whether I'm alone or with others. Drumming calls me into trance within minutes.

For any trance work using shamanic drumming, you should go into it with a purpose in mind unless you are asking the spirits to tell you whatever they think you need to know. Since you have a purpose here, you will want to spend a little time before the drumming to focus on your quest.

I always recommend casting a Circle of protection before you begin to drum, whether alone or with others. I'll explain why in a little while. Since the focus of the drumming in this context is to meet your totems, you might set up an altar using antlers, horns, bits of fur, pictures of various animals, statues of animals, and so on. If you had a different goal, you would change your altar's contents correspondingly. Or you might choose to simply meditate on your goal for a brief time and make your request to the gods. You can also drink some tea (mugwort is a good choice) or have a sip of a magical tincture to enhance your ability to slide into trance. I do not recommend drugs or too much alcohol for several reasons:

* Many of the drugs are illegal, and, trust me, you don't want to spend your totem-searching time in jail.

* Most drugs cloud the mind rather than open it up, and some are very harmful.

* The drugs that are used for shamanic experiences should only be used under the trained guidance of a medicine man or woman, be they of a specific tradition or not.

✳ You may not know how your body will react to a drug, and you do not want a medical emergency going on while you're drifting around in trance.

✳ Drugs can make you vulnerable to outside entities, making you unable to prevent any negative and unwanted visitor from bothering you while you are in trance; there are entities who are looking for a cosmic joyride, so to speak.

A little wine or some properly prepared magical tinctures may help induce trancelike states. Too much and you're just going to get drunk. The best high, and over the years I've experienced a variety of types including the chemically induced kind, is the magical high that comes from ecstatic trance and dance work. These forms of ecstatic communion make all outwardly induced highs pale by comparison.

During the drumming, whether you are drumming or someone else is, let your mind drift into the beat, and let the voice of the drum speak to you. If you are in a drumming circle, let the drums band together and talk. I've heard them, my friends have heard them, Samwise has heard them—it's especially noticeable when you are dancing or just listening as you let yourself drift along the energy. The drums have an underlying voice, and if you slide into an alpha-rhythm hypnotic state, you can often hear them singing. Sometimes the words are audible, sometimes the message is a primal, arcane chant . . . but it's there. I believe these spirits are singing through the drums to us, reminding us of things we have long ago left behind, things that we need to remember.

This is one of the reasons I recommend casting a Circle of protection before shamanic drumming—these spirits are very real and they do enter through the drums; most are fascinating and benign, but there are some astral entities that can be hard to deal with, and you don't want them interrupting your ritual, especially when you are attempting trance work.

If you've asked for a specific focus while drumming, you may find yourself pulled along into a guided journey. Close your eyes and follow the visions that come to you. If you've asked to meet your totems, a guide may appear to help you do just that. If an animal appears, talk to it—ask it what it needs to show you. Chances are, this line of questioning will open the gate for a longer journey rather than simply asking, "Are you my totem?"

When we are working with spirits, be they animal, human, or another astral entity, we tend to overlook the fact that if they have come for our benefit and truly seek to aid us, they will make us work rather than give us easy and pat answers. No self-respecting guide or guru will tell their acolytes everything they need to know, and the same holds true for spirit guides. They aren't here to give us a clear path through life, but rather to prepare us to navigate our own path, including the twists, turns, and obstacles that we will undoubtedly encounter.

Our animal totem spirits are part of our natures; we key into their strengths and weaknesses to learn more about ourselves and our lives, not to make life an easy jaunt. The process of discovering what and who our totems are should be an exciting journey, not just "pay the woman ten dollars and get a psychic totem reading."

Dancing to Meet Your Totems

In addition to drumming, we can often uncover our totems through magical dance. This can be done in two ways—one to discover the totem, the other to celebrate and strengthen it.

You will want to choose music that resonates within you. I recommend a good beat and few or no lyrics so as not to influence and distract the mind. Three of the best musical groups I've found for this kind of dancing are Gabrielle Roth & The Mirrors, Corvus Corax, and Dead Can Dance. Dead Can Dance is very gothic in tone, with a lot of hypnotic, Middle Eastern–sounding chants. Corvus Corax is a German medieval-industrial rock group; their music is perfect for ritual. Gabrielle Roth & The Mirrors tends to focus on aboriginal world-beat music and is my first choice.

If you can gather drummers together, you can dance to live drumming, though one of the main complaints I have about this is that often the drummers swing into a beat that is not necessarily the rhythm best suited to your needs at the moment. I would rather dance with drums when I don't have a magical focus and simply want to lose myself in the music, or listen to drums as a wonderful background for spiritual journeying.

Again, when invoking spirits of any kind—be they animal, human, or other—I recommend casting a Circle of protection before starting your ritual. This will give you a strong measure of safety and can help loosen your inhibitions when you start to raise energy. It's a good idea to warm up first so you don't hurt your muscles during the dancing. Keep water around—you don't want to get dehydrated during your dance. After you have warmed up, spend a few moments in silent meditation, much like you did with the drumming, asking for your totem animals to express themselves through your body as you dance.

When you begin to dance, if you are in a Circle with others, the hardest thing to do is to forget that the other people are there (obviously you don't want to go bumping into them, but it's vital to free yourself from any self-consciousness so you can sink into the energy and not distance yourself from it). Focus solely on your energy unless one of the other participants indicates they need help.

Let the music swell up through your body; follow the notes, follow one instrument, or follow the rhythm or harmony. As you continue dancing, you may find that you want to express yourself in a certain way. Your steps may become lumbering like a bear; your movements may become sinuous like a snake; your arms may extend like the wings of a bird, soaring. If you find yourself dancing an animal, don't try to analyze it; encourage it to fully come out through your movements. You will be able to tell which animal it is—no one I know of has danced an animal and not known what it was.

Enjoy the movement; allow your body time to play with these sensations. There will be plenty of time after your dancing to sit and think about what you learned from and about your totem animals.

Meditating on Your Totems

Guided journeys are a good method for discovering the nature of your totems. Make sure you have plenty of time. Guided meditations—indeed, trance work of any kind—should never be rushed. Settle into a chair and relax, or stretch out on your bed with the lights low. Bring your breath into a slow, rhythmic state, but not so deep that you hyperventilate.

Lowering yourself into the *alpha state*, as it's called in biofeedback, will increase your ability to visualize and work in trance, so your goal should be to hover in that semidozy state that exists between waking and sleeping.

You should also perfect your control of progressive relaxation (which I cover in my book *Crafting the Body Divine*) and work the tensions out from your body so you can focus without distraction. I don't recommend anything other than light music at this point, since drumbeats raise the heart rate, and for this type of work, you want to slow down your sensations.

As you drift into the alpha state, picture yourself standing in a meadow during the middle of the night with the moon shining overhead. There is plenty of light with which to see, and you are comfortable, neither too warm nor too cold.

Raise your arms and call out, "Spirits of the Earth, Spirits of the Air, Spirits of the Fire and Water, hear me. Spirits of the Land, Spirits of the Wind, Spirits of the Sea hear me. Bring to me the animal totem guides with whom I am to work. Let me see the truth of their nature, of my nature."

Then watch and wait for any signs of animals appearing in the meadow with you. If one does, don't immediately embrace it; instead, ask, "What do I need to learn from you?" and see what the animal has to say.

If nothing appears, then repeat your request and wait a while longer. If nothing happens, then this method will take some time for you to perfect or you aren't supposed to know your totem yet. Try again another day, perhaps under the new moon or on a day when you are feeling particularly relaxed and refreshed. If nothing happens on either of those days, then move on to another method for discovering your totems.

As with any trance work or meditation, come fully out of the hypnotic state afterward and ground yourself by eating something—preferably some fruit and a little protein. Do not drive or operate machinery immediately after working in trance—it's not a safe idea.

Omens and Portents—Observing the Signs around You

Along with the more magical methods of discovering what your personal totems are, there are several signs to look for when you begin your quest. When you formally state an intent—such as "I want to know what my animal totems are"—the Universe will most likely pay attention. You just have to know how to read the signs that it gives you for answers.

"Synchronicity" is a term that refers to things that happen within a short period of time and which are all interrelated. Most often the occurrences are for the good, and they usually happen in response to a need or energy that we have put forth.

This can happen when calling for your totems. When you begin to search for your totems, or when they decide it's time to manifest, you will most likely begin noticing stories, advertisements, pictures, television shows, books, and so on about or concerning a specific animal. You might pick up a *Discover* magazine, see an article on cane toads, and find yourself thinking, "Wow, didn't I just read about cane toads in *Audubon*? Here they are again!"

Or perhaps a sighting of the animal coincides with an important event.

Gawen says, "The owl came to me a few days before I pledged myself to Gwyn ap Nudd, the Welsh God of Death and the Fey. An owl flew over my circle just after sunset during the ritual and landed in a nearby tree. It sat there, watching me for the rest of the ritual, and it hooted as I was releasing the elements. Then it flew off. It was then that I knew that Owl was one of my totem animals."

Abbey had an even more tangible response to her request for a sign.

She says, "My totem animal is Coyote. I had been working with coyote magic for a few years, and I really couldn't determine whether or not Coyote was my spirit animal totem. To make a long story short, I was at Circle Sanctuary for the 1999 Samhain festival. A friend and I hiked up this large cliff called Spirit Rock at about one in the morning. While we were looking at the stars, I could hear two coyotes (from opposite directions). Finally, I just thought, 'Damn it, Coyote! If you're my spirit animal then give me a sign!' Just then, about ten coyotes all howled at the same time in the valley below Spirit Rock. Needless to say, I was totally amazed, awestruck. I finally had a positive answer! I was also a little scared because I had to hike back to camp, and instead of two coyotes nearby, I had a pack to think about."

If, for example, you believe Crow might be your totem but you aren't sure, ask for a sign from the crows you meet outside. You just might get one. You may also find yourself spontaneously dreaming about the animal, quite apart from the dreaming exercises presented earlier. As I recounted in chapter 1, I have had several dreams of my panther and boa totems, all mystical and beautiful. I've also had glimpses of the animals walking beside me, on the astral plane.

Creating Your Personal Vision Quest Ritual

While you should never attempt to use an aboriginal ritual as it is used within that specific culture unless you are led by one of their shamans, you can create your own vision quest ritual that works for you.

Many traditions stress hardship, physical endurance, and stamina as necessary attributes in order to achieve what is considered an honor or badge that you have completed a right of passage. In some ways, I agree with this. Anything truly worth having usually isn't easy to come by. On the other hand, you shouldn't be foolhardy and endanger yourself in your quest for spiritual enlightenment unless you are being led by a very experienced guide who knows what he or she is doing. Even then, you must know for a fact that you are in good shape and can handle whatever ordeals you're setting your sights on.

However, you can create a vision quest to challenge you without putting yourself in jeopardy.

What I am going to present here is a suggested ritual only. It is up to you to hone it to meet your specific needs. Obviously, if you are disabled or have medical problems that prevent some of the elements involved, then you must adapt it to meet your own needs. Physical perfection is *not* a requisite for spiritual enlightenment. Never let yourself fall into the trap of thinking, "Gee, because I can't go hiking and sit in the woods all night, I'm not worthy of having an animal totem."

And don't think that because your body isn't sleek and swift, your totem can't be. I am neither svelte nor fast moving, yet two of my totems live in the treetops (the panther often lurks in the trees, waiting for her next meal). But ask me to climb a tree in the state I'm in? I don't think so! However, that doesn't preclude my spirit from connecting with those animal spirits.

Here are my suggestions for creating vision quests. First, always take a friend with you in case you run into trouble, or at the very least, carry a cell phone and make sure it will work where you are going. If you head into the wilderness alone, you must remain alert. There are many dangers in the woods, human predators not the least of them. You never know whom you are going to meet. Remember to pack spare clothing and food in case the weather turns bad. Tell someone where you are going. In other words, please don't be stupid. Anybody idiotic enough to run off alone, without the proper supplies, without telling a friend where they are going, deserves to get lost and hungry for a little while. And if I were an animal guide, I'd be laughing my head off and refuse to show up to such a person until they learned to take better care of themselves.

Second, find a spot to where you can journey and camp out for one or two nights. You might prefer the beach to the mountains, or perhaps you have friends who have acreage that they'd be happy to let you park your tent on for a few days. This latter is an excellent idea if you can swing it. Your friends will understand what you are trying to do, and they won't swarm around you, asking questions. For some reason, strangers often seem feel they have the right to interrupt you when you're out hiking or camping. So decide how long you want to make your quest and where you want to go.

Don't stretch the quest out too long or you may get tired and lose interest when the mosquitoes get too bad. Yet, half a day isn't likely to produce the results you are looking for. A three- or four-day camping trip should give you enough time to relax and perform your ritual without feeling antsy.

Once you have set up camp, you should spend your first day relaxing—letting go of the mundane world. You and your friend can take leisurely walks, go swimming if the weather is good, fish, take pictures . . . play happy camper without worrying too much about what is ahead. Toward evening, you may want to begin preparing for your quest. The following is an example of what I might want to do on such a trip. As I said, adapt as necessary.

Sample Vision Quest

Tracy asks her friend Peter to join her on her vision quest. He agrees. They decide to go to a nearby campground, which is next to a lake. It's warm enough to enjoy the trip, but not yet warm enough for everybody to be descending on the park, and most of the camping spots are empty. Peter and Tracy wait for the night before the full moon to go, since she has an affinity with the moon. Armed with plenty of food and supplies, they drive to the lake where they set up their camp.

They've decided to take two tents—one for their supplies and for Peter to sleep in, and a smaller one in case Tracy needs a space to be alone and protected from the elements. Tracy has decided to fast for a day or two before the vision quest, and she is in a slightly altered state of consciousness, so Peter does the driving.

The first day, they wander around to get the feel of the park and the lake. It's a lovely area, wooded with thick undergrowth. Tracy notes a few patches of stinging nettle, and they remember the locations so they won't inadvertently wander into the plant. She is allergic and would require a doctor's care if she fell into a patch. She also makes a note to avoid one of the paths down to the lake since it is rocky; she recently turned her ankle and still needs to be careful putting too much strain on it.

Peter has brought books and a Walkman to keep his attention so he doesn't bother Tracy while she's searching for her animal totems.

The first night Peter makes dinner, and Tracy—still fasting—abstains from eating, though she does accept a cup of chamomile tea and a serving of a tincture designed to promote psychic awareness. She takes a flashlight, though she doesn't turn it on, her small handheld drum, and a walking staff and heads off to the lake. There, she finds a nice spot to rest as she listens to the gentle lapping of the water against the shore. The moon is rising, and she falls into a deep trance while watching it.

Peter has agreed to keep an eye on her from a distance, checking on her every half hour or so to make sure she's still there, unharmed. He doesn't come close enough to interfere with her psychic work or to startle her, but he does make sure that nobody is bothering her.

Tracy takes out the little drum and begins to beat out a rhythm, focusing on weaving the sound to match the pulsing of her heart. She gets up and casts a Circle next to the lake, calling out the elements and inviting the animal spirits to dance with her. For the next half hour she drums and dances, letting her conscious mind drift as her subconscious takes over. Peter checks on her a couple of times, but he is sure to keep his distance.

At some point, Tracy spontaneously sets down her drum. She picks up her walking staff and goes wading in the water under the rising full moon, basking in the energy crackling through the night. While no animal totems present themselves to her, she doesn't worry, but just enjoys the experience of the moment. After a while she returns to the bank, dries her feet, and leans back to watch the stars. Eventually she returns to camp, and she and Peter crawl into the tent and sleep.

Early the next morning, Tracy is woken up by a commotion outside in the treetops. She sees a hawk staring at her and feels some spark of connection; she knows that the hawk is not her totem, but he has brought her some sort of message. He flies toward a stand of trees nearby and she follows him.

After she has been walking along a path for about fifteen minutes, the hawk lands in a tree, shrieks once, and then speeds away faster than Tracy can follow. Tracy looks around the tree and finds a feather laying at the base—she's not sure what kind of bird it belongs to, but her fingers tingle when she picks it up, and she feels a spark of recognition.

She tucks the feather away and returns to camp, where Peter is making his breakfast. Hungry, she feels a gnawing emptiness from her fast, but she decides to hold out for a bit longer. Peter makes her a cup of tea and encourages her to drink some juice. He can see she's a little wobbly, and she agrees. The juice seems to help her a little, and so while Peter goes fishing, Tracy spends the morning in a quiet meditation. During the afternoon, Peter goes hiking while Tracy writes in her journal and naps.

That evening Tracy returns to the lake and casts another Circle. Peter again keeps watch from a distance. This time Tracy enters a deep trance brought on by the introspection, the environment, and the fasting. She feels the entire forest watching her; she can sense movement everywhere, and the lake takes on a mystical quality—a personality that both frightens her and beckons her with its deep mysteries.

As she stands, watching the waters ripple in the evening breeze, a shadow crosses her in the rising moonlight and a long hoot whispers through the air. She looks up to see an owl landing in the tree near her Circle, and immediately she feels pulled to the bird, transfixed. With that certain inner knowing we get when something is completely right, Tracy knows the owl is her totem. She also realizes that the feather she found earlier in the day belongs to the owl.

She greets the bird and watches it for a while, then it flies off with a final circling flight over her head. While it imparted no great wisdom, she knows that she will come to learn its secrets as time progresses, and she feels akin to the owl in a way that she never has to another animal. She thanks the spirits of the forest and returns to the campground where Peter makes her a cup of soup and some crackers so she can break her fast. That night, she sleeps soundly. In the morning they eat a good breakfast and pack up their gear.

Tracy will spend the next few months studying about owls and learning all she can about them as she welcomes her totem spirit into her space.

As I said before, if you are devising a vision quest of your own, you must adapt it so that it works for you. Perhaps you cannot sleep on the ground due to a bad back, but you can rent a little cabin somewhere and sleep in a bed. Or maybe you don't have access to a campground, but you do have the ability to spend a few days in a nearby county or state park, returning to your apartment at night. If you cannot light a bonfire due to zoning regulations then don't light one.

Use your imagination and come up with something truly personal and meaningful. The spirits will respect that far more than if you pay five hundred dollars for a two-day workshop where some guru you've never met before tells you what your power animals are and what they mean.

In Summation

The path you design for discovering your totem or totems may be complex or simple. But the totems will only manifest when it is the right time. You might need only to ask, and boom—there they'll be standing in front of you, large as life. You may even know them on an instinctive basis and won't need to do an extensive search. The animal will come to you in a flash, and you'll sit there going, "Okay, so you're my totem!" Or it may take months to discover which animals are connected to your soul.

Once you have found your totem(s), you can begin developing a relationship with them and then incorporate their teachings into your daily life. It may take you a while to fully determine what animals you have a resonance with, but once you do, the bond can be as familiar as the bond between a physical pet and the human they own.

The most common trait of all primitive peoples is a reverence for the life-giving earth, and the Native American shared this elemental ethic: The land was alive to his loving touch, and he, its son, was brother to all creatures.

—Stewart Lee Udall, *The Quiet Crisis and the Next Generation*

The Eye of the Peacock:
Observation and Nature

Tuning into the Natural World

After we have discerned what our animal totems are, it follows that we will want to know more about them and their attributes. While there are many good books that give overviews of the mystical significance of various animals, I always think that the best and first place to turn for information is nature herself.

When we observe a creature in its natural habitat, whether through books or television, or if we are lucky enough to spot our totems in the wild, we can form a better connection with them. Other options can provide satisfactory interaction as well.

Sharing Our Lives with Our Totems

For some totem spirits, we can integrate the actual animal into our lives and learn from it through constant physical interaction.

Please note that I am adamantly opposed to the private owning of wild animals—lions, tigers, wolves, and so forth need their freedom. They aren't domesticated, and it's simply wrong to keep them as house pets. Not only does it rob the animal of its wild dignity, but it also puts your family at risk because, like it or not, that cute baby tiger is going to grow up into a six-hundred-plus-pound wild animal capable of hunting you down and making you his lunch. This is the basic, unchangeable nature of tigers. They are predators, as are all of the big cats. Their instincts and drives make it impossible to give them the life they need in an urban situation. They have the primal urge to hunt, and they may not differentiate between your child and a young animal that would normally be their quarry.

Wolves are another wild animal that many misguided souls try to keep as house pets. They are not domesticated canines, and captivity can produce disastrous consequences for the animals.

Wolves require a wide range for their territory, and, again, they are predators, born to hunt, and they are not suited for adoption. Wolf hybrids are theoretically carefully licensed in most states, but the reality is that many halfbreeds slip through. Wolf hybrids are not always half and half, and they may have a majority of genes from their doggy ancestors or from the wolf side of the equation. Your best bet, if you want a wolflike dog, is to look into breeds like the Alaskan husky or the malamute, both of which have a similar look but are quite adaptable to household living.

Zoos and wildlife rescue houses are filled with the results of human ignorance and an unwillingness to check our egos at the door. These rescued creatures can't be returned to their wild state. They've grown up in captivity and haven't learn the proper hunting skills to survive on their own. Yet they are feral and do not integrate into human households, so must forever stay behind bars and in preserves.

Big snakes are another danger. There have been cases where large constrictors have killed their owners or their owners' pets. Snakes don't view the world the way we do, and we have to be cautious when approaching them from our very human perspective.

On the other hand, animals such as dogs, cats, pigs, rabbits, and ferrets *can* add a wonderful contribution to your family and are quite suited to interaction with human beings. If your totem is one of these animals, you have the opportunity to bring a real one into your home.

We share our lives with four cats at this point; they are part of our family and have their own responsibilities and their own individual quirks. Pakhit keeps Luna and Meerclar in line. Tara is my office cat and shares my writing life with me. Luna is our "problem child," but we love her all the more for her special needs. Meerclar is the entertainer of the bunch and delights in playing the clown. While my totem is the panther and not the domestic house cat, being around all the feline energy certainly enlivens Panther's maternal instincts, and I am fully fueled with what I call "caternal" instincts toward my furry felines. But I don't try to humanize them by interfering with their natural hierarchy, and whenever possible, I allow them to interact and spat and argue and play as they will. Pakhit is our dominant matriarch, Luna is second in command, and Meerclar knows her place at the rear end of the marching order. We keep Tara separate due to personality problems between her and Luna.

Cats seem to sense where they are welcome, and they know that cat energy abounds in my home. If I had Wolf as a totem, dogs would probably take up running through my yard, instead.

When we live with an animal, we get the chance to look, in depth, into its psyche—if we choose to learn from them. The animal will have its own personality. It will also have the traits that belong to its species. Day-to-day observation of an animal's moods and actions can bring us much closer to understanding what it means to share this planet with other species. And should we be observing an animal that matches our totem animal spirit, then we can also learn more about ourselves.

Starspirit's other totem, besides the red-tailed hawk, is the rabbit. She shares her life with two Dutch dwarf rabbits and says, "I have always been connected to rabbits. I had one as a pet when I was a child. I have often been the surrogate mama to little bunnies who lost their mothers, nursing them until they are out on their own. Presently I have the privilege of being the protector and provider for two dwarf rabbits that are happily bounding around our family room as I write this. I have a special connection to them. I know what they feel, what they need, and when they will let no one else touch or hold them, they allow me to pet them and they jump into my lap. From observing them, I gain an understanding of how to think quickly and use my intelligence. I have never known a stupid rabbit."

Wren shares her home with a raven named Hemlock. From this bird she learns patience, how to be in the moment and not rush life along to the next milestone.

While not quite sure whether he is a totem or guardian, Wren says, "Since reading Yas's requests for stories of animal totems or spirit animal guardians, I've been thinking a lot about whether Hemlock could be called either of these things. He's definitely here to teach, but it's a hands-on experience. He's a guardian like no other, dive-bombing those with whom he feels discomfort. He's so full of play that one can't help but be reminded of the excitement of taking each moment as the gift that it is. Upon first meeting, he will sit atop one's head if he's allowed, feeling the energy of the individual. If he likes it, he'll ease to the shoulder and feel your words, your breath. But busy as he is, never a day goes by that he doesn't sit atop the maple tree for a time, loving the sun, wind, or rain in silence."

If your totem is the dog, then you can learn more about what it means to be part of that canine energy by simply observing your pet, by interacting with him, and by putting yourself in the position of perceiving the world through your dog's eyes. Some of Dog's spirit qualities are loyalty, protectiveness, and pack behavior. You can watch your dog and then yourself, noting how you react in terms of loyalty toward friends and family, how you protect that which is yours—be it on the material or emotional level—and how you fulfill your needs for companionship. While those are the standard meanings, you may also find more subtle dog qualities that serve you well.

As I said above, while the house cat is not my totem, it most definitely embodies feline energy. I can learn about Panther on a limited scale through watching my own cats. One thing that isn't often mentioned when discussing Cat's energy is that, while solitary beings, if they have an attachment to someone, cats will provide comfort when that person is in pain. When I've been in pain, be it emotional or physical, my cats have milled around my feet, staring at me with worried expressions. Soon, one of them will come sit with me and try to distract me, especially if the pain seems very bad. So too, I notice that while I tend to gloss over superficial problems, when a friend or loved one is having a hard time, I become anxious, wanting to be there to help.

Totems and Animal Spirits in the Wild

Depending on where we live, we may have the opportunity to observe our totems in the wild. In my area of the country it is common to see squirrels, deer, rabbits, hawks, crows, opossums, harbor seals, herons, and even occasional foxes and coyotes in fields and forests. We have mountain lions around here too, but they are elusive, thank gods, for they are often shot by people who don't know any better. Bears are known to show up in a number of communities around here too, and if you go out on the tour boats, you can often see whales during specific times of the year.

You might want to study a regional wildlife guide or consult your local Audubon chapter to ask what animals frequent your area. Of course, it can be dangerous to tromp out in the woods in search of a bear, but you can safely observe some animals from a distance.

We have a lot of harbor seals in the bays and inlets around here, and I love watching them play. Their joy in life is apparent from their antics; they truly frolic and seem to enjoy doing so. If they were one of my totems, I would probably really tune into a playful "I'm alive" nature. As it is, I experience pleasure in watching them revel in their own lives.

Outside my office window (a spare bedroom in the house we rent), I see a number of squirrels on a daily basis. They are plentiful here and race up and down the trees that stand next to the outer walls of the house. They run along the fence and fight and chatter. Now and then I look up to see one staring in the window at me, intent upon some squirrel purpose that remains elusive to my understanding. I've even watched them mating on the fence. Again, Squirrel is not my totem, but by watching squirrels over the past four years that we've lived in this house, I've come to understand a lot about their cycles and inner nature. I understand squirrel medicine a lot more than I did before.

Squirrels are brilliant creatures, smart and funny and cunning. They like to tease the dogs and cats in the neighborhood and seem to really enjoy playing the part of the nosy neighbor. Territorial, they chatter angrily at anyone who dares to interrupt them. Through observing them I come to understand the need for attention to detail—they are very detail oriented in everything from how they eat a nut to how they hold their front paws. I can also learn from their intense scrutiny. They are good animals for writers to take note of because squirrels seem to observe everything that goes on around them. So while they are not one of my totems, they have been an animal guide and I've benefited from the time I spend watching them.

When we observe our totems in the wild, we often find some aspects of their nature disconcerting. Gawen has Egret as well as Owl for his totem. He often goes out to a lake nearby his home to watch them, and while they help him relax and learn to pace his life, he was at first startled by the sounds they make. This incongruity helped him realize something about his life, though.

"Watching the egret, I feel more able to take time away from the hustle and bustle of life, to relax and just enjoy my being. Whenever I work with Egret I feel at peace with myself, like nothing else matters. Egrets have a beautiful body and are very graceful, but if you ever hear them make a sound, they sound nothing like they look. Their call is a low-pitched, loud squawk. It's very hard to describe. When they let out these sounds when I'm meditating it's very unsettling, which suggests to me that no matter how at peace or serene I may feel, I always have to come back to reality."

For many, totem work is based solely in the mystical realm. For others, it becomes a living, breathing connection, and for still others it is a guidance system on a tangible level. My friend Andrew hunts to fill his freezer for food, not for sport. He is a fisherman extraordinaire and understands nature on an intrinsic level that many of us would love to experience. Yet, it is because he does understand his environment on this level that he is devoid of the light and love aspects many people ascribe to the natural world, people who haven't had firsthand experience in the harsh realities that are part of the ever-revolving cycles of life. During his teen years, Andrew went on a walkabout in the Yukon, alone with his ferret. It was during this time that his Raven totem made an appearance.

"I had a ferret with me, and we were both starving, not having any idea of reality-based hunting at that time. I was book-learned, with no viable help. The ravens used to come down and laugh at us. One in particular decided to brave the ferret, who usually would have gone for anything with wings and eaten it. The raven would wake us both up by sitting outside the tent, easily within arm's reach. He would watch us and talk to us. Just gossip-type stuff, 'How 'ya doing' sort of thing. Still, as long as they followed me, which was from the moment I got off the Greyhound bus in Muncho Lake all the way to Fairbanks, nothing bad happened.

"After I got to Fairbanks, they were not nearly as friendly, hanging back and laughing most of the time. It was in Whitehorse that they disappeared for some reason. There, I seemed to leave reality behind and entered some sort of alternate space where all sorts of strange, inexplicable, and bad stuff started happening. I'm not sure that I passed whatever test was thrown at me there. Raven has an irritating sense of humor if you don't understand his jokes. To Raven, everything is funny, which I guess is true if you view the cosmos as one big joke. It hampers his ability, though, if he really wants to get involved with humans. We see things as a lot more serious than he does, which begs the question only answered in hindsight, *Who is right?*

"It is not a malicious humor, though. You just have to keep laughing along with him despite the pain. 'Oh come on, it's not that bad' is a running theme, said laughingly. If you fail to keep a sense of humor, you run the risk of him leaving you for a while. 'What a drag, man, lighten up and I'll be back.'"

A few years ago, Andrew was taught a valuable lesson through his interactions with the Spirit of the Coyote. At that time, he and his wife were out hunting. They had split up for better results, when Andrew noticed a coyote watching him. He was impatient to get on with his hunt, and he raised his rifle, scoped out the coyote, then stopped. The coyote was resting in the grass, staring straight at him. It was an easy shot, but a connection had been made, and he let go the trigger.

He says, "I was still peering through the scope when I said (both aloud and mentally), 'Bang, you're dead. You owe me your life.' It seemed then that the coyote heard me because it stood up and 'said,' 'Okay, so now what?' I asked to be shown the buck I was hunting. Almost immediately the buck appeared, and I aimed, shot, and missed. The buck ran off, as did the coyote. Ravens flew over, and I sent a thought to them for help. 'Sure thing,' they replied, with much laughter. I kept on hunting. Pretty soon I came across another coyote. I repeated my performance from earlier, and again was given directions to the buck. I promptly lost him, this time for good. Heading back to the rendezvous point to meet my wife, I met yet a third coyote and again demanded a favor in return for its life. It must have been getting tired though, as was I, because I was told 'tomorrow.'"

Andrew and his wife met and went back to their camp. There, his lesson proceeded in earnest.

"Shedding our packs and gear, I then discovered that the keys I had thought to be in my pocket were still in the ignition of the truck, and there were no spares to be found. The magnetic key box with the spare keys that I normally kept inside the bumper had fallen out. I tried everything to get inside the truck, and eventually ended up smashing my feet through the back window by accident while trying to pop it out. It was getting dark by this point so we lit a lantern. While we were cleaning up, I noticed something burning. Somehow the shirts that we were supposed to wear the next day had come into contact with the lantern and had caught on fire. As we put the flames out, our dinner started to burn and was so bad that even the coyotes who hung around the edge of the camp waiting for food wouldn't touch it."

It was at this point that it all began to register, and both Andrew and his wife understood what was going on.

"Throughout this whole affair, I had a sense of being laughed at by Coyote. We could both actually hear him. These were little reminders to be careful when requesting help from him. There's always a price and, often as not, despite seeming to have the upper hand, we don't. I decided that after that, if I wanted help with the hunt, I should ask the spirits of the animals I was hunting, respectfully as did our ancestors, instead of adopting the threats and bullying so often passed off as requests with today's less-than-respectful attitudes. The result was a sacrifice in money, and finally a trial by pain when I got my elk tattoo. It has not gotten me an elk yet, but I do not expect it to. It serves as a permanent reminder to approach the spirits of the animals with respect, and maybe then they will offer themselves."

Game Parks and Reserves

There are some animal totems that most of us will never be able to see in the wild, but there are places where we can catch a glimpse of them. While I have a problem with traditional zoos because of the inhumane way in which they cage the animals—small cramped quarters and no natural surroundings—many zoos across the country are changing their ways and becoming much more animal friendly.

Game parks also provide a chance to observe many animals. Driving through a preserve may not be the same thing as seeing an animal in the wild, but the conditions in these compounds are usually much more amenable in the animal's natural habitat than a zoo, and they provide a measure of freedom for exercise and movement. They are fascinating places and give us a chance to interact with the animal kingdom in ways which we might never otherwise have. However, it might require patience on your part. If the mountain lion wants to go hide in a den, the groundskeepers are not going to prod it out for your inspection.

Many preserves house animals who were kept as pets until they grew too big to handle, or who were causing problems in communities. Rather than shooting these large animals, officials caught them and transferred them to the parks.

Bones, Fur, and Feathers

Another way that we can connect with our animal totems is by keeping part of the actual animal around. Now I am *not* recommending that you go out hunting for black-market animal furs and so on; however, I do think that in a religious context, we can honor and revere the remains that are left after an animal is killed or dies.

The elk skull that houses our house guardian, Krikki, is a good example. It may not be my totem, but Elk is our house guardian and is connected to Mielikki. I don't personally possess any part of my black panther totem and have to make do with pictures, nor do I have a green boa skin though I do have various skins shed from other snakes. However, I have a plethora of peacock feathers and use them in a number of ways, including masks, spell work, and wands.

Be aware: In some states, it is illegal to possess certain feathers and other items, and you should keep this in mind when you have the opportunity to gather them, so you can make a conscious choice about how far you are willing to go. I have been gifted with hawk feathers and owl feathers and other items. I treat them with as much honor as I can. However, I have my limits. If I knew that someone had killed a rare animal in danger of becoming extinct to sell the parts on the black market, I'd turn them in as quick as I could pick up the phone.

I rescue furs from secondhand shops if I want to work with the fur of some animal, and I give them honor beyond just wearing them for adornment. Since the animal is already dead, I can give some energy back to that spirit through sympathetic magic. Powwows are also good places to find furs and antlers. I have wolf fur for Tapio and bear fur for Mielikki, and I use rabbit fur and other leather in my magical work.

One day I found a dead seal on the beach. It wasn't clear what had killed it, though it didn't look like any human was responsible. I wanted to honor its death and life in some fashion, and so I asked the Spirit of the Seal if I could have a couple of its whiskers for my magical wands. I got the sense that my request was accepted, and so I clipped a few of its whiskers and took them home to use in making my magical tools. If I could have taken a couple of teeth I would have, but there were a few people wandering the beach and I didn't want them to call the cops on me, thinking I had something to do with the animal's death.

I paint bones to honor animals, and I make magical tools out of them. I seem to attract bones and skulls like some macabre magnet. I have no qualms about bringing home birds who have been the victims of roadkill and honoring their spirits by using their wings or bones in my art and magic. The rest of their body, I offer up to the woods, back to the food chain that sustains us all.

When discussing the use of animal parts in magic, we cannot help but come to the subject of hunting and animal sacrifice. I never tell people they have to eat meat to be happy or healthy. However, I will not allow militant vegetarians to browbeat me for eating and enjoying meat. I have no problem with hunting to fill the larder and keeping livestock in a righteous manner, but I would never kill an animal for any reason other than food or in self-defense.

Samwise and I are not vegetarians, far from it. I tried it years ago, and it didn't work for my body. When we buy our meat, we buy from a butcher rather than from the store. The beef from our butcher is raised hormone free. We also buy organic eggs. This is important, if you can afford it, because these animals are usually kept in more humane conditions, and the food is better for your body, having no dangerous additives.

Kosher laws demand a ritual form of slaughter for food animals to calm the spirit of the animal and prevent their fear from going into the meat. To me, this signifies a respect toward the animal that we don't see in regular slaughterhouses.

When asked, I honestly have to say that I don't see anything substantially wrong with some of the Santeria and Voudoun traditions that demand animal sacrifice, as long they eat the chicken being offered to the gods. I do, however, maintain that if you kill an animal in a ritualistic manner, it had better be one you've raised and not somebody else's pet duck, and you'd better do so in a humane and quick manner.

This is a touchy subject, I know, and while I respect others' opinions, I maintain my own stance. I am the Priestess of a goddess of the Hunt and a god of the Forest. Both Mielikki and Tapio were, and still are, approached by hunters asking help with finding their game. I see this as an intrinsic connection to the balance—it falls into the shadow side of the Craft, which is necessary for wholeness and balance.

If you have a predatory animal totem, you can't ignore the hunting instinct inherent within the animal, nor can you pick and choose which aspects you find acceptable and dismiss the rest. You must accept the animal's nature in full.

Andrew, introduced earlier, hunts to feed his family. He works directly with his Elk totem through the blood of the deer that he kills and carries on native-like traditions of working with the animals during his hunts.

"I hunt for elk, and so wear a tattoo that I feed with blood from the deer in hopes of communicating or getting hints on what to do while out there. So far I've had some interesting dreams, but Elk still remains elusive. I salute Raven, Heron, and Kingfisher whenever I see them, of course, as I would any friend. I even at times invoke their aid when hunting or fishing, promising choice leavings in return for success. I am usually rewarded and express my gratitude with offerings of gut piles, bones, and such from the deer carcasses for Raven. I leave dead bullfrogs for Heron. Kingfisher wants nothing from me, but I paint him occasionally and include his image on my spears."

Working with the animal spirits, we inevitably encounter death. Animals are part of the life cycle, as are we, and death is the natural culmination of life. We must approach this in a balanced manner, understanding the natural order in which the animals live, and the mystical connections they have to the Otherworld.

These connections were recognized and accepted by most native and aboriginal traditions, and it is up to us to learn about and accept them too.

Unfortunately, Western culture has removed death from life, through boxing it up in a pretty polished cabinet that promises to keep the loved one safe. (I'd like to ask, safe from what? By the time the funeral comes along, the spirit is no longer residing in the body.) We talk about "passing away" or "going to sleep" or "eternal rest" rather than "dying." But nothing lives forever; even the Earth herself will fade away when her time is up. We must accept the shadows of life along with the light and see that death is a transition that does not kill the spirit but, instead, frees it to move on in its evolution—not only for humans, but also for our animal friends, totems, and guides.

Books and Television

When we cannot interact with our totems in the flesh, we can learn about them by watching nature shows and reading books and articles written about them. If Gorilla or Chimpanzee is your totem, the perfect author for you to read is Jane

Goodall, the preeminent scientist in the field of primate ape behavior. Or you might want to take a look at Dian Fossey's work.

It's important to remember that just because you read studies based on a naturalist's point of view, you do not have to negate your mystical quest for understanding. One of my very favorite books, *Pilgrim at Tinker Creek*, was written by naturalist Annie Dillard, and through her work she taught me how to observe nature, how to really look into the core. Dillard's no more a Witch than the Pope is, but she is a mystic in her own right.

There are a number of programs on public television that give intimate and fascinating glimpses into the world of animals. *Nature* is one such series, *Nova* is another. The Discovery Channel offers *Wild Discovery,* and the Animal Planet Channel is filled with interesting tidbits. If you don't have cable television, you can rent some of these documentaries in video stores or check them out from some library systems.

The library is probably your best resource for learning about animals and their actions, but don't overlook the bookstores. Some bookstores have huge sections on animal behavior as well as picture books. Used bookstores can offer you substantial savings if you can't afford new ones. There are a number of magazines that offer glimpses into the natural world as well. Go to your local bookstore or magazine shop and peruse the shelves. I was amazed when I found journals devoted solely to snakes, amphibians, and so on.

In Summation

By studying your totem animals in their natural states, you can gain an insight into the mystical nature of their magic and their medicine that would elude you if you relied solely on texts offering only metaphor and symbolism. We can only go so far when relying on archetypal symbols of animals, for they are—after all—living, breathing beings, and even when in spirit form, they have a feral and wild nature. They are an integral part of the natural world around us.

I can call spirits from the vasty deep.

—William Shakespeare, *King Henry IV, Part III*

Astral Guides and Guardians:
Denizens of the Otherworld

What Exactly Are Animal Spirits?

Depending on which cultural reference you consult, the answer to this will vary. I must stress the following, however: These spirits are very real entities. They are not a figment of your imagination. Don't ever take them for granted, and don't treat them lightly or irreverently.

Some cultures believe that animal spirits are not really the spirits of animals, but that they are spirits who take animal form. In Mesoamerican native lore, the *nagual* is a spirit guardian believed to inhabit the body of an animal. The methods for forming a connection to the *nagual* varies depending upon what region you live in. In Korea, the mountain spirits are guardians called Sansin and are strongly associated with tigers. The Sansin are celebrated in hopes of encouraging them to drive away evil and bring good harvests to the farmers.

Other cultures and traditions believe that animal spirits are the spirits of dead animals, and still others maintain that an animal spirit comes from the essential Spirit of that animal species, much like I explained in chapter 2.

Will we ever know? Probably not. Does it matter at this point? Probably not. What does matter is how we interact with these spirits and that we never, ever take the word of an astral entity over our own common sense. In other words, if you have a wolf for an animal guide and it tells you to go sleep with your neighbor's wife, I don't recommend taking its advice. The spirits and gods often test us to see whether we have learned to think for ourselves, and most of them— at least most of the beneficent ones—don't want sheep for followers; they want to interact with humans who are developing in their spiritual lives. By never questioning advice, by never thinking for ourselves, we do not evolve, only blindly obey.

Thinking for ourselves is one of the biggest advantages, as well as disadvantages, that Pagans have. We don't follow an arcane book of rules that has only changed through mistranslation and corruption by greedy officials as do many religions grounded in dogma. Pagans should look to the past, but live in the present and adapt accordingly. We follow our instincts, our inner guidance, and the guidance of our guides and gods. We weigh the options and are required to think instead of simply react. It's up to us to make sure that we stay on our path, yet it is also up to us to make sure that the path that we are walking is the right one for our personal beliefs. This requires taking personal responsibility for our actions and deeds, as well as for our misdeeds.

Having said that, where do *I* think animal guides and guardians come from? In my opinion, our totem spirits are avatars of the Spirits of the (fill in the blank) essential energies. My Panther is an avatar of the overall Panther Spirit. I believe that household guardians and astral spirits like Krikki are avatars of the energy they embody. Krikki is both an avatar of the Spirit of the Elk and an embodiment of protective energy. He is a specific entity, a manifestation that comes from the Spirit of the Elk; therefore, he is, indeed, an elk spirit. Has he ever been on the physical plane as a live elk? I don't know.

We also find the occasional animal spirit that has been in animal form on this planet. One Samhain, Samwise and I were holding our usual dumb feast when a little kitten spirit showed up in the room. The kitten didn't know she was dead, and I could actually feel her crawl up on my lap. I did my best to embrace her, to send loving thoughts to the little thing—she couldn't have been more than eight weeks old when she died—and then I called on Mielikki to come escort the kitten away to the other side. My Lady appeared, and I felt her gently pick up the kitten and carry it with her. I started to cry because it was both so beautiful and so sad, and my eyes still tear up when I think about it.

My mother felt our cat Eek come to her after the cat died. I was long gone, had left for my junior year of college. One night shortly after Eek died, Mom felt the covers on the bed shift. Eek used to sleep between her and my stepfather and sure enough, the blankets were moving as the cat's spirit walked up between them and laid down.

Making Contact: In Our Dreams

In our sleeping states we often have interactions with animals who aren't our totems. They may come into our dreams when we need to learn lessons from them, they may appear to help us over rough spots in our lives, or they may be bringing us a message from the gods. Sometimes these encounters can be disconcerting and in a few cases, downright frightening.

Spider is always trying to teach me lessons, but I have pretty strong arachnophobia and, in my dreams, Spider comes not as a helper, but as a purveyor of obscurity, filling the houses in my dreams with such thick webbing and so many thousands of her kind that I am paralyzed with fear, unable to move or see my way through the tangled webs that completely take over the rooms. If I move, I'm terrified that a spider will crawl on me or that I'll get caught in the webs and never get out. I believe, since the house in question is always my childhood home, that she's reminding me of the complexity of the abuse issues that surround my childhood and how they have affected me and still do affect me.

Ginger often dreams of animals who come to guide her through some of life's travails. Sometimes she dreams of her loved ones as animal spirits. When her father was dying, she says, "I dreamt of being in an Indian village up in the mountains where everyone was happy, working and playing. I made a comment to a woman about how beautiful life was there, and she said, 'You should see our place on the other side, it's even more beautiful.' There was a commotion where people were gathered around a well. A large deer was trying to go down the well, but it had gotten stuck and was frightened.

"I reached out and grabbed its ear, trying to hold it still, but it slipped out of my hands and disappeared down the well. Somehow, I pulled the ear off, and when I opened my hand, it had turned into a medicine bag. I believe the deer was my father, and the message was to be gentle and not be frightened. Then I woke up. He had been in denial about his dying up until he heard I was coming home, and then he admitted for the first time that he was dying. I told him not to be afraid. He said he wasn't but that we had to be patient. I knew this was a message for me, since patience has always been my bane."

It could be that Deer was her father's totem and that by leaving her a part of himself—the medicine bag that had been his ear—he left her a gift. It is up to Ginger to figure out what the message is. Quite possibly, what her father gave her in the dream is symbolic of what he gave her at her conception: the gift of life.

Since we often use our dream states to work out problems or to examine hidden fears, it shouldn't surprise us when astral guides and guardians show up to help us better understand the issues that are facing us in our waking lives. As Witches, as shamanic journeyers, as healers and metaphysicians, we must examine all aspects of our own lives, including the hidden fears that lie within the depths of our psyches. If we cannot turn inward and wander the labyrinth that leads to our own core, complete with the monsters we create from our fears, then we will never be able to face the energies with which we propose to work.

When we are open, instinct takes over and we find ourselves working in our dreams, examining our lives through kaleidoscopic microscopes. Unfortunately for most of us, the dream state can warp and disproportion our worries, which is why it's better to meet these problems head-on instead of letting our subconscious attempt the job. The animal guides we work with in the dream state may do the best they can but, as with my fear of spiders, it doesn't help if we fail to understand their purpose in being there because we're recoiling in fear. No matter how many times I have had that nightmare, I never have been able to stop and understand what spider is trying to tell me while still in the dream. I always wake up in panic, on the verge of screaming.

Making Contact: On the Astral Level

Animal spirits may confront us during our waking states, while we are working on the astral level. We may be meditating, working at our desks, exercising, or just wandering around our house when we get a psychic glimpse of a spirit, and we can either allow ourselves to pull into the experience and see what the spirit wants or shake it off as a flight of fancy.

Karri, a writer and artist, was getting a healing session from a psychic worker. She says, "After an hour of energy balancing and chakra work, my healer was standing behind me, working at my head. I was emerging from a deep meditative state when I felt a sudden shift in the energy flow. A dark shape appeared and quickly formed into the head of a black panther, his golden eyes burning bright. He shifted, restless. I waited, thinking, 'What does he want with me?' As soon as the thought formed in my mind, he leapt into me. Disoriented, I took a deep breath, surrendering as his body fully entered mine. The healer was still working in silence, massaging the base of my skull. As his hands moved forward to press and rub behind my ears, the panther purred in delight. As if on cue, the healer began to massage my head vigorously. That cat was in ecstasy! As the healer finished the massage and stepped back, the panther disappeared. When I could finally speak, I turned to the healer. 'So,' I asked, 'do you have an animal totem?' His eyes widened. 'I'm not sure. Someone once told me that I have a spirit guide, probably a jaguar or a panther. Why?' I laughed and said, 'Well, he just introduced himself to me.'"

As I said before, Samwise and I have a house guardian spirit that is an ancient elk—Krikki. I believe that Tapio decided we needed him and so brought him to us. Until I was given an elk skull, I had no plans to summon up a house guardian. Then, once I had the skull, it hit me out of the blue that we *would* have a guardian spirit and it *would* be housed in the elk skull. When we performed the ritual, Tapio was right there and he ushered Krikki in, so I think it was a setup; it is one that I'm quite happy with—but I still think it was decided without my opinion.

For Youngtree, Wolf's appearance on the astral realm manifested to him through a photograph. The astral image managed to be caught on film and spoke to him as if he'd first sensed it as a spirit.

"I'd been raving for weeks, and I was at a Pagan gathering when someone took a picture of me with one of those instant cameras. As the photo developed, a strange red 'lozenge' was the first thing to appear, bisected by a transverse green 'lozenge.' I went over and stood where the picture had been taken from, trying to figure out what could be making the odd blotch appear on the film. As the picture continued developing, the shadow of a wolf's head resolved itself on a tree trunk above and behind me, and the colored blotches were its one eye. It was immediately apparent to me that Odin, in his wolf aspect, was calling to me. I made my pledge to him on the spot. Over the years since then, this totemic aspect of Odin has revealed what this means to me and who I am. Wolf is my primary warrior mode."

Most of us are likely to encounter animal spirits while in a waking trance state. When we are working in trance, when we are working with meditation, we are open to the astral and etheric realms. We are tuned in, listening for signs and symbols during these times and have readied ourselves for some sort of contact. The trance state is also the most likely state from which we will be summoning animal guides and guardians. It is vital to remember, and I cannot stress this enough, when we go wandering on the astral plane, we are encountering very real entities and these journeys are not simply flights of fancy or daydreams.

Most shamanistic cultures believe wholeheartedly in spirits, and they do not wish to offend those spirits with whom they make contact. To write these spirits off as constructs or symbols and relegate them to the realm of archetype is very disrespectful. When we ask for help from the spirits, or when they offer it unbidden, we should tender respect in return. Modern Paganism often looks at ritual and symbolism without exploring the ancient traditions and foundations on which these rituals are based. By doing so, we lose the substance of the act and only keep the shell.

While our animal guides and guardians may not require an offering—we are a part of them rather than existing separate and distinct from them—often house guardians or guides will want something in return for their troubles. For example, Krikki asked for apples and leaves. We keep a basket hanging near the fireplace filled with apples and replenish them before they get mushy. These fruits are his, and no one eats them; when we remove them from the basket, we always replace them with fresh ones. We can sense him eating them on an energy level. If we looked at him as simply a mental construct, we would not be leaving fruit around for him, and he would probably become offended and leave.

Making Contact: In the Flesh

Sometimes a specific animal will come into our lives on a physical level to be a guide, teaching us lessons we need to learn and interacting with us in our magic. At times we call them "familiars," which is the subject for a separate book. Other times they are guardians for a period in our lives when we need their energy to protect us.

The night I first met the Goddess, way back in 1980, a mangy cat followed me all over campus on my walk. I'm still not sure who this cat was, but it was definitely linked to my experience. (Read the full story in *Embracing the Moon*.) I think, perhaps, it was a test to see whether I'd pay attention to the signs that the Lady was giving me that night before she made her appearance. If I had ignored that poor love-starved and bedraggled cat, would the Goddess have called me back into her service? If I had pushed away the cat, would she have pushed me away? Perhaps not, but I think it was a test to see how compassionate I was, how much I really cared about my fellow creatures.

Wren's raven, Hemlock, whom we met in chapter 4, came to her first as a foundling. A fluke? Perhaps, but that this bird should show up on her doorstep seems no coincidence when considering the Goddess that Wren works with.

"Over a decade ago I was called into service by Hecate. She taught me not to be so analytical, how to speak Truth. She taught me the simplicity of living a magical life. She continues to teach me today, as I enter Cronehood and embrace it for the joy and freedom it brings. It was no surprise to learn that Raven belongs to Hecate."

About nine months before Wren told me this story, a man cut down a tree on his property without realizing that there was a two-week-old raven in a nest lodged in the branches. A mutual friend called Wren and told her about the baby bird and asked if she'd take it.

She agreed and says, "He arrived in a dog crate, nestled in a towel and some shredded paper. He had to be the ugliest little thing I'd ever seen, with fuzzy feathers clinging here and there and a huge wide mouth that 'acked' and 'cawed' constantly. We established his place and began to learn his needs. Bugs, worms, wild bird formula, tiny feeding implements . . . all became household knick-knacks, while washcloths by the dozens were tossed into the laundry in lieu of diapers. Thank gods he slept through the night, as he ate every waking hour those first few weeks!

"Before long, I was taking him to the garden to explore and learn where his food comes from. The sooner I could get him to the worms, the better. Hemlock is about nine months old now, and he's not your average raven. He lives freely, able to enter and leave the house at will whenever the door is open. He sleeps most nights perched on a door or the four-poster bed. He chooses to stay out at night only when the moon is full or there's a big storm to experience."

In some cases, we undergo a rite or ritual at an animal's hands. One of her totems, rather than an animal spirit, claimed Angel Winges in the same way that animals mark their territory, and elks were used to deliver a powerful message to her from the Gods. She was in Fern Canyon, where the movie *Jurassic Park* was filmed, performing a morning ritual when a herd of elk joined her.

She says, "Several years ago on Lughnasadh weekend, I went camping with some friends at Fern Canyon. We were told to be very careful when we checked in because it was rutting season, and the elk can be quite aggressive and hurt you. On the second morning, everyone wanted to walk the canyon. I wasn't able to because of my disability, so I chose to walk the beach trail instead.

"I first went to the dry creek bed and chose a couple of river rocks to make a tiny altar and do my morning devotional. When I finished, I turned around and about twenty feet from me stood a yearling bull elk. He looked at me, lowered his head, bent one front leg and 'bowed' to me. Then he quietly turned and walked away. I was stunned and felt deeply blessed by the Lady and the Horned Lord.

"Using my canes, I slowly walked the trail through the trees close to the beach. I came upon a lovely little glade where seven elk cows were grazing. They were beautiful. They walked as they grazed and were headed for the tree line. Elk cows form a matriarchal society. The only time the bulls are allowed to be in the herd is during rutting season. Outside that time, all but the yearlings have a separate herd from the cows.

"I watched the elk cows fade away into the trees. I then became aware of this wonderful aroma. Hawaiian flowers have a particular sweetness that I haven't found anywhere else, and even though this was California, the scent was reminiscent of Hawai'i. I spent a couple of minutes trying to locate the flowers before continuing on my walk. About five hundred yards further on, I rounded a curve and came upon a full-grown elder bull elk. He was huge—the rack of his horns was at least six feet across. The sight stopped me in my tracks. I'm only five feet tall, so he dwarfed me. I quickly focused a cloak of invisibility around myself and stood very still.

"Prior to this trip, I had been dealing with facing my Cronehood. I had turned fifty-five that year and was not at all pleased with the changes taking place in my body. I was very content with the wisdom aspect of Croning, but as a single woman, I was having a hard time accepting the physical changes.

"The elk began to bellow and shake his rack at me. I was standing on the path with the nearest trees being at least twenty feet away on either side of me. The closest cover was a large bush about three yards away. I very, very slowly began to edge toward the bush, intensifying my sense of invisibility. While I was so overcome with the beauty, size, and majesty of this animal that I barely had room for fear, I still knew that I needed to get a tree between us in case he charged me.

"He stood firm in his steps and made it very evident that he was 'courting' me. That stunned me. I was so awed that I could barely exercise my common

sense. I just wanted to walk up to him and hug him! Why would an elk be courting me?

"His bellowing and rack shaking began to escalate, and he walked to the
nearest tree and began to shake the branches repeatedly. He was quite vigorous
in his attempts to convince me that he was *the* bull of the herd and that I
should mate with no one else but him. By this time I had managed to get a bush
between us. I could still see him clearly. The bush offered no real protection, but
I felt safer.

"As the realization that he was truly courting me sank in, I was suddenly
struck with the understanding that this was the Horned Lord using the form of
a bull elk to give me a message. I was still a beautiful woman! At the age of fifty-
five, plumping belly, cellulite, wrinkles, and all, the Horned Lord found me
attractive enough to court me! When this hit home, I dropped to my knees.

"As I watched the elk—indeed, throughout the whole experience of the
morning with the yearling, the cows, and the bull—I saw a pattern taking shape.
During Lughnasadh, we enter the period of the Crone and the Holly King, a time
of aging and wisdom. Aging is not an ending, but rather a period of deep introspection and self-awareness that we go through each passing year; it is a time of
renewal and rebirth that culminates with Winter Solstice.

"I had just become a sacred Crone (an honorific term used in our tradition,
giving me the official title of 'Lady') within my Temple, and I was being physically acknowledged by the Lady and Lord in a most dramatic fashion. I was
stunned and honored, and also deliciously awakened by the erotic message from
the Horned Lord. It is an experience that will never dim in my memory."

She continues to find the Spirit of the Elk entering her life on a physical
level. "The largest herd in America of Roosevelt elk lives at the bottom of the
small mountain that I live on. They nap and graze next to the road. I stop and
talk to them frequently. I let them know I appreciate them protecting my kitties
(I have ten) from the predator critters on the mountain. I catch them up on the
news in my life, too, and let them know that I care. I feel the elk are mainly in my
life as protectors."

The animals who share our lives may act as guardians and guides, too. Whenever I have nightmares, Pakhit enters my dreams and tries to help me. Often, she'll wake me up from my bad dreams, batting my face with her paw until I shake out of it. Dogs often serve the role of guardian in our lives, and I believe that these loving and caring animal spirits interact with us on the physical level because we allow them into our hearts and our lives, because we connect with their natures and don't deny them their essential beings. There is a big difference between someone who "owns" a pet and someone who shares their life with an animal.

Some Common Questions Regarding Animal Spirits

Over the years, I've collected a number of questions that readers have asked me about everything from potato bugs to past-life connections with animals. Some questions dealt with the animal kingdom directly and the same theme has showed up enough that I have decided this would be a good place to provide some answers.

Can Pets and Other Animals Sense Ghosts and Spirits?

Yes. Most animals seem to be highly attuned to the astral plane and the Faerie Realm. Often, during ghost sightings, pets are recorded as yowling, howling, meowing, and running away to hide. Or they may sit in the doorway of a particular trouble spot and growl as if daring the spirit to come any closer. Animals are very sensitive to natural forces (such as earthquakes and storms) and supernatural forces. You might want to pay attention if your animal companion goes into this sort of behavior when there seems to be no logical explanation. Always check to see whether there's a mouse or a peculiar odor or something else that might set them off, but keep in mind that our animal companions have far more acute sensory organs than we humans.

If I Seem to Draw One Particular Type of Animal to Me, What Does That Mean?

Most likely this means that the animal species has something important to teach you. It doesn't always mean that the animal is meant to be your totem, or even that it will stay in your life as a guardian, but for a while at least it has shown up as a guide, and you'd do well to pay attention to what it might mean for you.

If I Have an Infestation of Potato Bugs, Does This Mean I'm Being Cursed?

This was an actual question that I received, though I have to say that the letter was spelled so poorly I could barely read the three-sentence, unsigned wonder. I will admit, I was having a rough day, and receiving letters like this makes me wince. I wrote back (via email) and told her that no, it meant she should keep her house cleaner and consult her local pest authority.

Insects are hard to place in the role of animal guides and helpers. While they do have their attributes, the fact that they are so prevalent and so plentiful on the planet means we have to be cautious when ascribing a mystical meaning to swarms that might invade our space. And if we are poor housekeepers, chances are, our answer lies with the more frequent use of a dust mop and a trash bag.

However, if you are *dreaming* of insects, the chances of it being a message from the Otherworld are much higher. And if you live in an area where, say, beetles are rare and you suddenly find them by the hundreds in your yard and house, then you might want to examine the possibility of it being a spiritual message that you need to decipher.

I Seem to Have a "Ghost" Cat or Dog Running around My Place. Why Is It Attracted to Me?

Just as with humans, when an animal dies it may not realize that it's dead. Sometimes animals are so attached to the places they lived that they will travel hundreds of miles after their family moves to return to the house they are used to living in. I believe it's the same when an animal dies. If they aren't ready to move on, if they don't realize they're dead, then they may return to the place where they lived because it is familiar and comfortable to them. You might also attract a wandering animal spirit who misses its human companion and wants that loving connection again. In cases like this, it's best to invoke a deity who works with the particular species in question. Ask the deity to help the lost spirit over to the other side where it can be free to incarnate again.

I Have a Terrible Fear of (Insert Species). Does This Mean I Had a Bad Past-Life Experience Involving Them?

Not necessarily. Sometimes fears are brought on by childhood trauma, and we must always take a look at the psychological factors that go into fear. There are also studies being done on certain phobias to ascertain whether or not genetics play a part in these paralyzing fears.

When I was very young, I was terrified of bears, even though I loved my stuffed bears. I grew out of the fear and now, when I think back, I cannot find a specific origin for that fear, nor can I pinpoint the time when it stopped. It seemed to vanish as if it had never been there. However, my lifelong fear of spiders has never gone away and still interferes with my life in subtle but definite ways. I don't like sitting in the grass till I've scuffed through and convinced myself it's not full of jumping spiders. This is an improvement. I used to never sit on the ground at all due to my fear. I don't stay in the same room with a spider until someone catches it and either (yes, I know, bad medicine) kills it or puts it outside. I simply cannot sit in a room where a spider is crawling around on the ceiling above me; I'm always afraid it will drop on me. I no longer scream when I see a spider across the room, but I am antsy and itchy until it's gone, and sometimes I end up taking a shower to wash away the "itch" that comes when I see an especially large arachnid.

My spider fear goes back to childhood (though studies being done are showing the possibility that a fear of snakes or spiders maybe genetically programmed into some people as a self-defense mechanism). When I was little, we lived in a house with black widows in it. They were plentiful and so the words "danger" and "spider" were entwined for me. We also had tons of other spiders running around. Add to this the time when I was about seven years old and managed to tie myself in a chair with my jump rope so tight that I couldn't get loose and a spider dropped down from the ceiling to dangle in my face, and you've got the recipe for a phobia. It didn't help that when I screamed for help, my stepfather came in and yelled at me for tying myself up before he removed the spider from in front of my face.

So no, your fear does not necessarily point toward a past-life experience, though you shouldn't automatically rule this possibility out.

The Deity That I Work with Has Such-and-Such Totem. Does This Mean It Has to Be My Totem Spirit Too?

No, your totems will not necessarily be the same as your deities' totems, although their totems may come into your life more than some other animals might. I keep images of bees, stags, and wolves around for Mielikki and Tapio. Bear plays a big part in our spiritual lives since the Finns were considered to be part of the Euro-Asiatic Great Bear Cult. I work with Krikki, the elk guardian, even though he's not my totem.

You will have your own soul connections to animals, and they may or may not be the same as the soul connections your deities have to the animal kingdom. Most deities are connected with several animal spirits. We call these "correspondences" in westernized magic, but in the divine sense it really comes down to totem spirits. At times, if we work closely with a particular animal, we may also "pick up" on one of the deities it is close to. So you have to watch the interplay. Perhaps an animal spirit is coming into your life because a specific deity wants you to sit up and take notice of him or her. If Owl is suddenly a strong part of your life, you might want to think about Athena or some of the other gods that are linked to the owl, checking to see whether somebody isn't tapping you on the shoulder.

In Summation

There are many factors that play into why an animal guide or guardian spirit has chosen to enter our lives and how they go about introducing themselves. We can work with these spirits to protect our families, our energy, and our home environments. If we honor them in a respectful fashion, they may stay with us the rest of our lives and we just might find that they become beloved friends over the years. Samwise and I have grown very fond of Krikki, and we often sense him snuffling around, just being the protective and friendly elk spirit that he is.

Here there be dragons.

—Warning found on an ancient map

Fantabulous Beasts:
Working with "Mythological" Creatures

Dragons and Unicorns and Chimeras, Oh My!

"Cryptozoology": The search for actual proof leading to the discovery of creatures as yet undocumented by science. Cryptozoology is a controversial subject not only in the scientific realm, but also in the metaphysical and Pagan communities.

What it comes down to is this: Are these beasties real? Do dragons and unicorns and Nessie exist? Does Bigfoot wander the woods of the Pacific Northwest while his cousin, the yeti, climbs the Himalayas?

We have no proof either way, for sightings are rare, but science can't prove these creatures don't exist. The scientific community tends to believe that our ancestors who reported seeing these legendary creatures were looking at something else altogether; for example, ancient sailors seeing a mermaid were actually viewing manatees. Frankly, if someone has been at sea long enough to mistake a manatee for a half-woman/half-fish creature, then I think they really, really need shore leave.

What it comes down to is this: The majority of those of us who believe in these creatures seem to believe that they are from the Otherworld, and that they can enter our realm occasionally but don't generally reside here.

As I have said in my other books, I've seen a unicorn. I looked for all possible rationalizations. I wasn't stoned. After realizing that there was nothing to explain away the sighting, I accepted that yes, I saw a unicorn; therefore, yes—they exist. I don't ask that others blindly accept my word, but that they do accept that I believe I saw one.

In this book, and this chapter, however, we will treat these mythological beasts as real. For the sake of argument, and since I'm writing the book and this is what I believe, we'll go on the assumption that these beings exist in another dimension, one that intersects or overlaps our own. Interaction is much more likely on the astral level, but it can happen on the physical level also.

Working with these creatures differs to some degree from working with regular animal spirits and totems. For one thing, you don't stand much chance of going to your local zoo or game park and watching the beast in action. For another, there aren't any set texts that give the truth and nothing but the truth about them. We cannot begin to fathom all their mysteries. I may have seen a unicorn, but that doesn't make me an expert on them. We can search legend and myth, study all the different tales, and come to some basic conclusions, but we will never be able to fully comprehend the scope of their realm.

Mystical, Mythical Totems and the Physical World

Many people claim totems that are thought to exist only in faerie tales and mystical legends, yet these creatures have indeed been seen on the physical plane. My own entry into the Craft was preceded by the sighting of a unicorn. (Read the full story in *Embracing the Moon*.) I looked at it as a test—would I have the courage to believe my own eyes, or would I relegate the sighting to a hallucination and shake off the mystical side of life?

For a long time I prefaced my story with the words, "I know that this sounds incredible, but . . ." I don't bother with qualifiers anymore. I know what I saw.

I saw a unicorn in the woods one night. It was as real as I am. It looked at me, then vanished in front of my eyes. I believe that it came into this world from the Faerie Realm, just as I believe that faeries enter and exit our realm when they choose.

Many people in the world today are afraid to speak up and talk about their experiences. Some people have seen ghosts but can't talk about it. Others have seen supposedly mythological beasts and don't open their mouths for fear of being ridiculed by others, even by Pagans who profess a belief in the magical world.

I wouldn't be surprised if you have had one of these sightings and kept quiet about it. A number of people have written to me over the years about their experiences because they know I won't immediately scoff at them. After all, I saw a unicorn. I can't very well look at a letter and say, "Oh yeah, you saw a faerie, huh? I don't think so!" For I've also seen faeries, spirits, and other interesting denizens of the Otherworld. If you have seen such creatures, know that you are not alone. And chances are, you aren't crazy either.

Some people have managed to get a physical glimpse of mythical totem spirits. Among her other totems, which include the elk and the red-tailed hawk, Angel Winges also works with the Spirit of the Dragon. She is one of the few who has been lucky enough to spot an actual dragon on this plane. I have been corresponding with her for some time and am convinced that she saw exactly what she says she did.

She says, "Yas, I had the most fantastic experience on May 10 last year (2000). I have no curtains in my bedroom, so I can watch the stars from my bed. My bedroom faces the ocean so no one can see me. On May 10, I awoke to find myself staring at a baby dragon. She was hovering right outside my window. The body was about seven inches long and very slim, like we think of Asian dragons. The wings reminded me of hummingbird wings. She used her tail, which dipped way down, as a rudder for turning. No horns, etcetera, on her head. She had a really sweet little face and actually smiled at me before flying off and over the bar. I made a point of telling my doc in case I had something like a brain tumor though! But a real-life flesh-and-blood dragon . . . they're back!"

Here There Be Dragons

According to lore, ancient maps and globes included the phrase "Here There Be Dragons" at the edges of known territory, a warning to travelers that, beyond the indicated boundaries, danger awaited in the form of the unknown. I have researched this phenomenon, and it appears that far fewer maps actually bore this caveat than is commonly touted; in fact the Lenox globe (circa 1503–1507 CE) is the only globe known to bear that phrase. There are references to dragons on other maps, but very few are in the form of "Here There Be Dragons."

So what, exactly, is a dragon? According to the *American Heritage Dictionary,* a dragon is "a fabulous monster represented as a gigantic reptile having a lion's claws, the tail of a serpent, wings and a scaly skin." Other names for dragons include wyrm, firedrake, wurm, and "terrible serpents," all indicating the links between dragons and reptiles.

Dragons have been a pervasive symbol throughout just about every culture on this planet. In one form or another, people have been spotting them for thousands of years, and we seem to be closely aligned with them on a spiritual-evolutionary line. There are myriad forms of the draco family; Western dragons, Oriental dragons, serpents, and monsters are all connected with them but not fully dragonesque.

Oriental dragons are snakelike and wingless, with short legs and arms. Chinese dragons are said to have five toes, Korean dragons have four toes, and Japanese dragons have three toes. The Chinese word for dragon is *Lung,* and there are several different types, including:

* Tien-Lung (celestial dragons, who protect the Gods)

* Shen-Lung (spiritual dragons, who control wind, rain, and storms for the benefit of humanity)

* Ti-Lung (earth dragons, who control rivers)

* Fu-tsang Lung (dragons of the Underworld, who control and guard treasure, metals, and gems)

Dragons are found in a variety of colors, red and gold being two of the most common. Oriental dragons are seen as beneficent. Wise and intelligent, they make good use of their magic. But, if they are upset, they're thought to cause flooding and storms. The Chinese Dragon Kings, the Lung Wang, are ruled by Yuan-shi Tian-zong, the Celestial Venerable of the Primordial Beginning—one of the supreme deities of Taoism.

Westernized perceptions of dragons tend to be less generous with praise. Many dragons are seen as terrible beasts out to destroy humans, though dragons do have a long and venerable history in Celtic mythology. Indeed, the entire Arthurian saga is built upon the dragon. Merlin is said to have seen a great dragon appear in the sky and foretold Arthur's birth from that vision. The red dragon, originally brought over from Rome, became the standard for the Pendragon flag.

Dragon lore abounds in the British Isles, with one of the more famous tales being that of the Lambton Wyrm. During the time of the Crusades, John Lambton, a young member of the Lambton family, was out fishing on a Sunday morning. He caught a horrible-looking wyrm—an armless, wingless dragon. He threw it down a well and forgot about it. For seven years he was away from his village, fighting in the Crusades, and when he returned, he found that the wyrm had emerged from the well and was now a huge, vicious dragon that was scouring the countryside, eating cattle and killing anyone who got in its way. John asked a Witch how to best the wyrm, and she told him that if he killed the creature, he would also have to kill the next living thing he saw or invite disaster on his family.

John went to kill the dragon and managed to slay the beast. He then walked toward home, looking for the next living thing he would see, when his father came walking by. Unable to murder his own father, he did not fulfill the prophecy, and his family was cursed with untimely deaths for nine generations.

While there have been stories of good and generous dragons in westernized cultures, many more have been portrayed as sinister, greedy, and murderous.

Among the fiends we meet Jormungandr, the Midgard Serpent from Norse mythology. A child of the monster/god Loki and his wife, the giantess Angrboda,

Jormungandr spans the world, living deep in the ocean where he bites his own tail becoming, in essence, an oroborous.

There he waits until Ragnarok (Gotterdammerung, the Doom of the Gods, the apocalypse of the Norse cosmology). Then Jormungandr will shake the earth as he rises out of the sea and makes his way to land. His venom will fill the air, and this will signal the armies of the giants and the gods to engage in their final battle. Thor will overcome the dragon, yet it is predicted he will die doing so.

Among other malign dragonlike entities, we find the Grecian Hydra, a multiheaded dragon that, according to legend, could regenerate its heads when they were severed unless the central head was killed. The Hydra also possessed a terrible venom, and its breath was poisonous enough to kill anyone who came within reach. It attacked cattle and villagers until Heracles came to the rescue and beheaded the beast, burying it deep within the ground.

In Hindu legends, we meet Vritra, a dragon or serpent who was said to be so huge that he could surround mountains. His head soared into the sky. By gathering all of the world's waters into himself, he created a wasteland of drought and famine. When Indra, King of the Gods, was finally born, he attacked the demon. The two battled, with Indra railing against Vritra's ninety-nine fortresses. Eventually, Indra managed to destroy the dragon with a thunderbolt, and then he released the waters to flow back into the world again and replenish the land.

Dragons are reminiscent of reptiles, and reptiles and amphibians—ancient beings who have remained relatively unchanged since the time of the dinosaurs—exist within the Dreamtime lore. They carry secrets and stories from the beginning of time, and when we connect with one of their kind, be it crocodile or dragon, on a spiritual level, they may allow us to cajole them into telling us some of their stories.

If we are lucky enough to attract their attention (in a positive manner, of course—attracting the wrath of a dragon or crocodile spirit wouldn't be one of life's more joyous experiences, although it would most likely be memorable), then we should consider ourselves fortunate and pay attention to the lessons they have to teach us.

I work with an earth dragon for prosperity and abundance. She has chosen to stick around our home as one of the family, but this wasn't my doing. Unlike Krikki, I didn't summon her. She just showed up one day. Over five years ago, I was casting a series of prosperity spells—we desperately needed extra income—and I was very focused on the energy of abundance. One day as I was preparing my candle for a spell, I sensed something in the room with me. Something big. Very big. Sooooooo big. I didn't feel any threatening energy, so I tuned in to find out who or what was there. Now I've never been particularly drawn to dragons, so imagine my surprise when I found an old, large, green dragon in my office. If she had been on the physical plane, she would have knocked out the walls and ceiling.

Well, I didn't know quite what to say. It's not every day a dragon drops in. After a few minutes during which we examined one another—by now she knew I'd sensed her—I asked what she wanted. She said she had come to work with me for a while and that she was an earth dragon. I asked what she wanted to work on with me. She said wealth, prosperity, abundance, the material world. Well, it seemed like a good proposition to me, and since I sensed only positive energy from her, I agreed. Don't mistake me, though. I knew she could blast me out of that room if she wanted, and I was rather intimidated by the whole affair. I asked her what she wanted to be called and distinctly heard her say, "Emma."

Oh great, I thought. Emma the Earth Dragon. Maybe I'd misheard her? I asked again, "Are you certain that's the name you want to be called?"

Immediately, I was hit with a blast of impatience, almost like a huff, and once again heard her *very* firm words, "My name is *Emma*."

Emma it was and Emma it still is.

She's still with us. In most of my prosperity and materially focused spells aimed toward both ourselves and others, I ask for her help. I keep an altar for her with a lovely green dragon candle, a bunch of crystals, a dragon tarot deck, and a treasure box, because one thing I've learned that seems to play true about dragon lore is that they like their treasures.

I had a lovely silver box that my mother gave me years ago with Oriental dragons running around it. I gave this to Emma. It sits open on her altar, filled with trinkets and shiny things that are hers and hers alone. Every now and then I buy a little charm or crystal and add it to the box. She wants presents, and so presents I give her. She's very comforting to have around even if she is, at times, a little overpowering; so she and Krikki wander the astral realm in our home.

I've had several other experiences with dragons over the years. Friends who owned a Witchcraft shop summoned a dragon to protect their store. Before I knew they had done so, I was at the shop one day, standing by the counter when something big brushed my arm, much like a cat rubbing up against me. I felt a breath of hot air wash over me. Startled, I jumped.

My friends asked me what was wrong, and I told them something big had just rubbed up against me. That was when they told me that they had recently summoned a dragon to come watch over the shop. On the few occasions I watched the store for them when they were out of town, I sensed their dragon hanging around. He would wander around the shop, and he was obviously lonely for them because he got very talkative. I would find myself holding some pretty interesting discussions with him—aloud, no less. If anybody had walked in during one of those times, they would have found me jabbering away with nobody else in sight.

I am also a Reiki Mistress, and years ago, I formed an alternative branch of Reiki, which I call the Path of the Emerald Dragon. More Pagan-oriented than traditional Reiki, I've developed stories and information that I've culled from the spirit of the Emerald Dragon—a child of the God and Goddess. Basically, the Emerald Dragon is a part of the backbone of the Earth. This all ties in neatly with what I later learned is the Chinese view that the dragon's back forms the ley lines that run across the planet.

If you want to work with dragons, it would be a good idea to study up on their lore so you don't end up invoking a dragon spirit who might have a bad influence in your life. Although dragons, like all legends, are bound to be different from what we read in the books and stories, we can get a feel for the type of energy that certain "breeds," so to speak, will be like. For example, I ascertained, when I first met her, that Emma was wingless and that she seemed of a benevolent nature. From what I have read, I'd wager that she belongs to the Oriental dragon family, and she most likely is related to the Fu-tsang Lung dragons since she has such a love for and interest in the world of money, gems, crystals, and sparkly things.

Remember this: You do not control a dragon. Fiercely independent, they control themselves. If you are working with dragons as astral guardians or guides rather than totems, you should probably offer them something they like to encourage them to stick around. As I said, Emma has a treasure box on her altar, and what goes in there is hers. Should she ever choose to leave, I will take everything in that box and bury it somewhere in the woods or pour it into a river for her.

"And the Loveliest of All Was the Unicorn" (Sang the Irish Rovers)

The night I ended up staring face to face with a unicorn changed my life. I'd always half-believed in faeries, unicorns, and other such creatures, but to be standing there, gazing at the beast for real, pushed me over the edge into believer. Especially after I went crashing around the woods, looking for any possible logical explanation and came up empty-handed.

I consider myself blessed and fortunate to have seen such an incredible being, yet, like all gifts of this nature, it comes with a double-edged blade. When I decided I would talk about it and be honest, it left me open to ridicule from a number of skeptics—even Pagans and metaphysicians—who weren't willing to cross that line and accept that there might be something *real* about this magical business of ours. But that's okay. I understand the need to keep an open mind, to say, "I don't know if I can accept this unless I've seen it myself."

However, in my experience, the unicorn was as real as the computer upon which I am writing this book. And that is how I approach the subject in my work.

Unicorns are often equated with medieval tales and stories, but their history actually goes back to Mesopotamia where they were widely pictured in art. Then we find them in the Orient. In Japan, we have the Kirin, a godlike horned horse who rewards the righteous with good luck. The sight of a Kirin is an omen of extreme good fortune. The beast punishes the wicked with its horn and is considered a protector of the just and innocent. The Chinese call the unicorn the "Ki-lin," and they too personify it as good, caring, and compassionate. The Ki-lin lives in a paradise and is said to only visit this world at the birth of a wise philosopher. In Chinese mythology, the creature can live to be over a thousand years old, and it is commonly seen as a one-horned deer with an oxtail, horse hooves, and a fish-scaled body.

In 398 BCE, the Greek historian Ctesias, who believed unicorns lived in India, described them as "wild asses which are as big as a horse, even bigger. Their bodies are white, their heads dark red and their eyes are deep blue. They have a single horn on their forehead which is approximately half-a-meter long." This report is thought to have been based upon his viewing of rhinoceros bones and horns, but there were legends all over Asia of unicorns roaming the wilds.

Unicorn horn was believed to have many magical powers, including that of resurrecting the dead. During the Middle Ages, it was believed that only a virgin could tame a unicorn, and hunting plans called for such maidens to sit under trees, where the unicorn would come willingly and sleep in her lap and then the hunters could descend upon it and kill it.

I have received several letters from people who have seen unicorns, close in size and shape to the one I saw. Relieved, they spilled out their stories to me knowing that their secrets would be safe with me and that someone would believe them. Most of these encounters took place out in the woods, when the person was not expecting a mystical experience, and most of these encounters seemed to have a subtle but definite life-changing effect on the viewer.

It is my personal belief that the unicorn is from the Faerie Realm, and that it slips in and out of our dimension when it will. My interaction with it has been only the one sighting, and then years later in a dream. Shortly before I was called into the service of Mielikki and Tapio, I had a dream reliving the experience of seeing the unicorn. I heard someone telling me that the Goddess to whom I would pledge for life must be a Goddess who understood the nature of unicorns, and I heard the name "Mielikki." When I woke, it was as if I had seen the unicorn for a second time; the wonder and joy of that first night had swept back through me. And the unicorn led me to Mielikki, just as the unicorn first led me to the Great Mother Earth Goddess who welcomed me back to the path of the Witch.

Other Fantabulous Creatures

People occasionally choose to work with other creatures of legend and lore in their astral animal work. I am saving anything associated with the Faerie Realm (aside from my brief overview of the unicorn above) for another book, but the world is full of oddities that have never been explained.

The Sasquatch has never been fully understood or identified, though those of us who live in the Pacific Northwest take it seriously. Its name is derived from the Salish language and is thought to mean "wild man" or something similar. Some tribes refer to the Sasquatch as "Brother."

While the creature seems to be, at first glance, an urban legend, the lore of the Sasquatch goes back long before Caucasians came to this continent, and it is well documented in Native American myths. I wouldn't doubt that someone has been called upon by Sasquatch as one of their totems. If that is the case for you and you are looking for information, consult books on Native American lore for legends regarding the creature.

Nagas are part crocodile, part dragon. Intelligent creatures from the Hindu legends, they live in a watery region under the earth. Before working with them in astral form, I would caution the reader to do their research and know precisely what energies you are dealing with here. *Nagas* are connected with water (though it is said they will eventually destroy the world with fire), and they are often thought to be guardians and sentinels.

The phoenix, a mystical bird of fire and flame, comes originally from an Assyrian myth that found its way into Greece. The phoenix was also connected with the Egyptian city of Heliopolis. In Japan, these birds are called the *houou* and feed on the fruit of the bamboo. The bird caught fire every five hundred years, and a new bird sprang from the ashes, embodying the energy of regeneration and transformation. This seems like it might be more of an astral spirit to work with rather than a totem, but you never know who's going to be called by what spirit. The phoenix is a wonderful spirit to work with during times when transformation or regeneration is the focus.

We're all familiar with the Egyptian sphinx, but did you know that there are actually three types of sphinx: the androsphinx, with the body of a lion and the face of a human; the criosphinx, again a lion's body, but with the head of a ram; and the hierocosphinx, a lion's body with the head of a hawk. The sphinx embodies wisdom and reminds us that wisdom does not reside solely in human form. The sphinx carries hidden knowledge and obscure facts. By working with this creature's astral spirit, we can ferret out the information that we seek, but we must be observant enough to understand the answers. Not all advice or guidance comes in a blatant and direct manner.

The gryphon is another creature that is commonly referred to in mythological lore. Known as the hounds of Zeus, gryphons possess a lion's body, an eagle's head and claws, and long ears.

Also known as *griffon* and *griffin,* these creatures originate from ancient Asia. In Persia, their image was used widely in various art forms, and the gryphon symbolized wisdom and strength. It also represented the sun when it became the steed for Apollo in Grecian lore. Gryphons have long represented strength, alertness, and vigilance. Eventually their image was adopted by the Christian religion as a symbol of Jesus's ascension after his death and resurrection. When seeking to work with the gryphon on an astral level, honor, truth, and the search for wisdom and knowledge would seem to be requisites for successful interaction.

In Summation

There are numerous mythological beasts, some of whom are wandering the astral plane. If you wish to work with any of these spirits, be cautious and invoke them only for the energies that are aligned with their legends. Also, double-check all the sources you can; some mythological creatures have temperamental natures and, as we discussed, since these spirits are very real, you do not want to end up summoning someone or something that is going to cause havoc in your life.

The spirits that I summoned up
I now can't rid myself of.

—Wolfgang von Goethe, "The Sorcerer's Apprentice"

Invoking the Sentinels:
A Method for Summoning the Guardians and Guides

Think before You Invoke

Before you summon up any astral spirit—be it animal, human, or some other beastie—ask yourself why you want to do this. Why do you need to interact with this creature? There are many good reasons for calling on the animal spirits for help. These reasons do *not* include the following:

* because my friends will think I'm cool

* because I want to avoid doing any protection work for myself and, instead, I'll leave it to the spirits

* because I want control over other beings

* because I'm just experimenting and want to see what will happen; I don't really have a reason

* because Yasmine Galenorn told me I could

* because I can

There are, however, many legitimate reasons for invoking the animal spirits. Some of the better ones include:

* because my doors are locked and I've warded my house, but I still feel like I could use some extra protection

* because I want guidance and I've dreamt twice of an owl spirit coming to me to lead me on a journey, so now I want to invoke Owl and see what I can learn from him

* because instinct tells me I'm going to need extra strength in the near future, and I would feel better if Elk were on my side

* because my mother is dying and she's afraid, and I would like Bear to help lead her gently into the Underworld

* because I want to honor Bast and would like to give the Spirit of the Cat an honored place in my home and spiritual life

* because I'm working with the Worldwide Wildlife Association, and I would like strength from Tiger to help me as I work toward protecting his species

* because I know in my heart that I need to work with Horse and I want to understand the horse spirit while as I study it in physical life

Listen to your heart, your spirit, and your gut. If your reasons for invoking an animal spirit are valid, you will know it is the right thing to do. If your reasons are ego driven and likely to result in a bad experience, you should be able to fathom this out. And if you have delusions of controlling these animal spirits and won't keep yourself in check, then you probably deserve what you get, and I can pretty much guarantee it's not going to be a whole lot of fun.

Finding a Home Base for Your Sentinel

An animal spirit often needs a physical object to hone in on in the physical realm, much like a ship needs an anchor to steady it in the sea. This object is sometimes called a "host" or an "anchor." You can provide a host for a spirit in several ways. If you come across a skull of the particular species you're invoking, you can use that. You might check with taxidermy shops or butchers if you would like to go this route. You can also find interesting bones and horns in some secondhand shops and at flea markets, as well as at online auction houses. The Bone Room (www.boneroom.com) has a number of bones and skulls available for students and researchers. Other "hosts," or "homes," for the spirit include:

* statues of the animal

* candles in the animal's shape

* stuffed toys (yes, a stuffed toy will work fine—just don't let your child or pet get hold of it and run around with it)

* framed paintings or pictures of the animal

* a pendant or talisman in the animal's image, or a figurine—wood, clay, metal, or glass will all work just fine

* a collage of images that represent the animal

As you can see, a wide variety of objects are suitable to house the guardian or guide, and they will range in price from free (great-aunt Martha's tiger figurine she gave you as a kid) to pricey (a Waterford crystal statue of a dolphin).

You can buy modeling clay like Sculpty or Fimo and use that to make your own figurine if you like. Or perhaps you might carve an image out of wood if you have the talent. Making your own host for the spirit can intensify the bond between you. I'm not proficient in arts and crafts, though I am good at making masks of the gods. I find I do much better at hunting down the right home for a guardian spirit in a store.

When I have the chance, I love working with bones and skulls, and I had great fun preparing the elk skull we use for Krikki. I grew very connected to the spirit of the actual elk that had died. It was as if by preparing the skull, by cleaning it, staining it, and oiling it, I was honoring the original animal's spirit. In essence, I laid out the elk's remains much like people used to prepare their family members' bodies after death—with respect and love.

Don't overlook unusual objects for anchors or hosts, either. You might find an abstract sculpture that, for whatever reason, just screams the aspect of an animal to you. Or perhaps a black-light poster will work. In other words, be creative and listen to your own instinct.

Ritual Preparation of an Anchor (Host)

Perform this ritual preparation using only two or three steps.

First, physically clean the anchor. Be gentle, but thorough. Then let it rest for a brief time, preferably just a few hours.

Second, perform the spiritual cleansing and the warding in one step. You can invoke the spirit in a third step if you need to. However, the cleansing and warding need to be done on the same day in order to keep the magical energy flowing and to ensure that no other spirit takes up residence before you can invoke the guardian or guide. When you cleanse an object designated for magical use, you create a void. Any number of entities or energies can enter that void.

Therefore, if, due to time constraints, you must separate your magical preparation into two or three steps, cleanse and ward the anchor, let it rest, then come back to charm it.

Cleansing an Anchor for a Guardian or Guide

Once you have found a suitable anchor for the guide or guardian spirit, you will need to prepare it and get it ready for use. This involves physical cleaning, and psychic cleansing. This is one reason I like anchors that are made of bone or wood. They are quite amenable to oils, and magical oils make a wonderful addition to the spell work.

If the anchor that you've chosen has been used in any way—for example, an item from a thrift store or from your attic—then you must cleanse it on both the physical and psychic levels.

First, you will need to physically clean your anchor. If you can scrub it without hurting it, do so. Remember that crystal of any kind is best washed in lukewarm water; very hot or cold water could shatter it. If the object has been sitting in an extremely cold or hot spot, bring it to room temperature before you wash it.

If you can't wash the object in water, then dust it thoroughly, using a soft cloth to rub off any dirty spots. Skulls can usually be scrubbed, though I generally don't immerse them in water. I cleaned Krikki's elk skull by using a bowl of warm soapy water, a sponge, a Brillo pad, and a toothbrush.

If any parts of the item are loose, you might wish to fix them. I used white school glue to affix teeth back in the elk skull and reinforce some of the joints that had weakened due to sitting out in the weather for so many years. Check statues for weak parts, cracked legs, and so on, and take care of them now before you invoke the guardian into the host. Posters and pictures might need rematting or taping if there is a tear. With large animal-shaped candles, I always cut the wick down to the top so it can't be lit by mistake. Dust candles carefully, and keep them out of direct sunlight. If temperatures get too hot, you will need to place candles in the refrigerator to keep them from deforming or discoloring.

After you've physically cleaned and reinforced your anchor, you will need to cleanse it on a magical level, so get out your smudge stick. Just about anything can be smudged (as long as you aren't allergic to the smoke or herb). The smoke shouldn't hurt wood, crystal, paper, or clay (just don't let stray sparks burn up your painting or poster). Cast a Circle and invoke the elements. Light the smudge stick and say:

∼

Spirit of the Smoke, cleanse this anchor,
Prepare it for the guardian spirit,
Wipe clean lingering residues of past owners
And leave it new, cleansed, and protected.

∼

Thoroughly inundate the object with smoke as you visualize any residue from the past drifting away with the smoke. Try to get smoke into every crack and crevice. Take your time and be thorough; don't settle for a cursory job. After you are done, take a small broom (your magical broom will work, but a whisk broom is usually better because of its size), and sweep away the smoke from the object, removing the last remaining bits of stagnant energy.

If you are allergic to smoke, then you will need an alternative way of cleansing your anchor. One of the best alternatives I've used is "rattling" the object, which involves using a rattle to shake up the energy around an object or person. Your only concern here is that when the rattle takes over—and if you allow the energy of the rattle free rein, it usually will—you will want to avoid hitting and possibly injuring your anchor. You must keep alert when you are rattling the energy of something because, when you are working in trance, the rattle can move faster than your control.

Take the rattle—preferably one that you have worked with before—and slowly shake it around the edges of the object. Visualize the energy within the anchor breaking loose. As you rattle harder, the energy will begin to fly off and out of the general area. Essentially, you are shaking up the anchor's aura and this frees stagnant energies. When you feel you have rattled enough, and more often than not the rattle will let you know you are done by stopping on its own, take a small broom and gently sweep the energy away like you would with the smoke.

Always make sure your smudge stick is safely extinguished. You can place it, burning side down, into a bowl of salt or sand. This is an easy way to establish some safety standards in your magical practice.

Warding a Spirit Anchor

Once you have cleansed your anchor, you should ward it so it won't attract negative energies. For this part of the ritual, you will need:

* four white votive or taper candles firmly set into candle holders

* Algiz Oil or a similar protection oil and a thin bristle paintbrush

* a large sheet of paper that your anchor can easily fit on with room to spare

* a red and a black marker; alternatively, if you have it or can get it—
  Dragon's Blood ink, black ink made from a paste of oak soot and New
  Moon Water (burn a piece of oak in a fireplace until it's charred; scrape off
  the charcoal and mix it with a few drops of New Moon water to make a
  paste), and a feather quill

* your magical anchor

* a box of salt

* Protection Powder or a similar mixture of protective herbs

* an athame (or crystal or wand)

While still in the Circle from cleansing the anchor, invoke one of the deities that you work with regularly, or you can use this general invocation to the Lord and Lady:

~

Great Mother Goddess, Lady of Beasts,
Lord of the Forest and Hunt, I call upon you.
Be with me in my rites as I prepare this anchor
For the invocation of my animal spirit guardian.
Be with me in my rites as I protect and ward this anchor.
Strengthen my magic, shore up my power,
Protect me against all unwanted energies.
Be with me, Great Mother and Lord of the Wild,
Blessed Be, and Welcome.

~

After you have invoked the Lord and Lady (or whichever of the gods you choose to invoke; if you choose not to invoke deities, be sure to ask for a general blessing from the Universe), you are ready to ward the anchor.

Anoint the four white candles with the Algiz Oil, and let them dry.

On the center of the sheet of paper, use dragon's blood ink (if you don't have any, use a red marker) to draw a giant Algiz rune, which is the Norse rune of protection: ⅄. After this dries, use the oak-soot ink or a black marker to draw an invoking pentagram over the top of the rune.

When the ink on the paper is dry, trace both the rune and the pentagram (first the rune, then the pentagram) with Algiz Oil, using the paintbrush. Let the paper dry.

Set your anchor in the center of the rune and the pentagram on the paper. If amenable, anoint the anchor with Algiz Oil. If your anchor can't handle the oil, set a layer of tissue paper between the anchor and the paper.

Encircle your anchor and the paper with a ring of salt (if you do this on the carpet, you'll be sorry—try to find a place like the dining room table or a hardwood floor where you can sweep up the salt and herbs afterward). Then sprinkle Protection Powder in a circle over the ring of salt. Drop thirteen drops of Algiz Oil, evenly spaced, onto the ring of salt and herbs.

Set the four candles, one to each side, around your anchor and the paper, and light them.

Using your athame, or a crystal or wand, draw a sevenfold Circle of energy around the anchor and paper, visualizing the energy as you repeat this charm aloud:

~

First a ring of brilliant white,
The Maiden rides her stag tonight.
Second, a ring of blood-rose red,
The Mother rules the hearth and bed.
Third, a ring of black star-suns,
By Crone's own words, my will be done.
Fourth, a ring of Earthen brown,
Powers rising from the ground.
Fifth, a ring of mist and wind,

Clarity, the Air will send.
Sixth, a ring of flame and Fire,
The cone of power rises higher.
Seventh, a ring of Water blue,
May this spell's aim be strong and true.

~

When you are done, the air should be charged with energy; build it into a cone. Focus it into and around the anchor, repeating the three-word mantra of "protect and strengthen" as you direct the energy into your anchor for the spirit. When the energy slows down, you can either let the candles burn out and invoke the spirit later, or you can prepare for the invocation at this point.

ALGIZ OIL

Algiz Oil is a good, very strong protective oil blend, and it can be used in banishings, bindings, and other protection magic. Be sure to note the caution in the directions about use on skin.

> 1/4 ounce olive or almond oil
> 3 drops black pepper oil
> 3 drops cinnamon oil
> 5 drops rosemary or rose geranium oil
> 10 drops Dragon's Blood oil
> 5 drops High John the Conqueror oil
> A few crushed black peppercorns
> A chip of carnelian or ruby

In Circle, blend the oils. Add a few crushed black peppercorns and a chip of carnelian or ruby. Raise energy and charge, focusing protective and cleansing energy into the blend. Note: This oil may be irritating to your skin, so use caution; use an eyedropper to drop it on objects to be anointed and use an inexpensive paintbrush if you want to spread it around on objects. Store the mixture in a dark jar.

PROTECTION POWDER

Protection Powder can be sprinkled on doorsteps or windowsills or it can be put into a sachet and carried or tucked into the car for extra protection. Just remember: Never rely on magic for your sole support. You need to remain alert and use your common sense. Use dried herbs and resins for this recipe.

> $1/4$ cup wormwood
> $1/4$ cup basil
> $1/4$ cup dill
> 2 tablespoons peppercorns, crushed
> 2 tablespoons rosemary
> 2 tablespoons frankincense resins
> $1/2$ cup salt
> 1 crushed oak leaf or 1 slivered holly leaf (holly has sharp edges, be careful)
> $1/2$ cup cedar needles

In Circle, blend all the ingredients using your hands or a mortar and pestle. Raise energy and charge, focusing on protective energy radiating into the herbal mixture. Store the mixture in a dark jar.

Invoking a Spirit into Your Anchor

You are now ready to invoke a spirit into your anchor. How you go about this will depend on what kind of animal spirit you are summoning into your life, and for what purpose. If you are summoning an animal guardian, your intention will be to invite them into your home to protect both your home and all who dwell within its walls. If you are invoking an animal guide, you will be calling on the spirit for more personal help—specifically to guide you in your spiritual quests—so you will have to tailor the invocation to your needs.

When you write your invocation—for you will be the one writing it—there are several factors to take into consideration. You should:

* Always be polite, none of this "Spirit come here to my command" crap. Attitudes like that get you in trouble.

* Be cautious about how you word things, especially if you are working with the Spirit of Coyote, Raven, or another trickster animal. You could be in for some unexpected shocks if you don't say exactly what you mean.

* Be specific about what you are asking them to do. For example, ask them to guide you during spiritual journeys or guard the house and all inhabitants; don't leave your request open-ended.

* Never throw in something extra that you just thought of when you are in Circle. This impulsive behavior gets a lot of people in trouble, and I'm guilty of it myself. That little plug for abundance when invoking Bear for protection may turn into abundance in the form of a pregnancy since Bear works so strongly with the mothering instincts.

* Be sure you have done enough meditation and journey work to know what the animal spirit wants in return. *Never, ever* make out a blank check on the spiritual level. This is both stupid and dangerous, and if you do something like this, be prepared to pay a high price. I did once, and I paid for many years through hard lessons. And if, for example, the horse spirit you are going to work with wants apples and carrots, have an apple and carrot ready for the ritual.

* Postpone the summoning if something feels wrong as you are writing out your invocation until you have thoroughly meditated on what you are doing.

* Remember that we are working with the animal spirits, in conjunction with them, and we do not control them nor do we allow them to control us. Always keep this in mind when you word an invocation or work in the metaphysical realm.

Let's use the example of someone summoning a wolf guardian for her home. We'll call our Witch Mariana. She's had five years of experience in the Craft, is an eclectic who listens to her intuition, has read widely, and is now working with totem spirits and animal guardians. Mariana has had four dreams of wolves coming into her space, protecting her and her family. She has had good interactions with friends' dogs, and this mirrors her connection with the Spirit of the Canine. After much thought, she's decided to invoke a wolf guardian for her home, and her meditations have shown her this is a good idea and that the Wolf would like to be given a soft spot in which to stay. Mariana has prepared a small box filled with soft rugs and placed it near.

She comes across a lovely statue of a wolf and buys it, taking it home where she smudges and wards it. Now she's ready to invoke the Spirit of the Wolf to enter her anchor and become part of the family. While in Circle, Mariana takes a deep breath and opens up her psychic sight. She reaches out with her senses, searching for the Spirit of the Wolf, summoning it to her. When she wrote her invocation, she was very careful in her wording, and she starts to chant the words as she searches with her higher self for the guardian spirit.

"Spirit of the Wolf, come to me, spirit of the great Northern wastes, you whose howling at the moon can be heard in the hearts of all Witches, you who protects your pack, your family, you who embody the spirit of loyalty. Wolf Master, Pack Leader, I call thee to come to our home, to take your place in our family as guardian and sentinel against all entities and energies we find unwelcome.

"Spirit of the Wolf, spirit of the icy snows and endless forests where the tree-tops kiss the heavens, where lights flicker in the starlit sky, Spirit of the Wolf, we invoke thee and ask you to be with us. Guard over our family, guard the very walls of this home, keep watch as you walk through our halls, be our friend as well as our guardian. Help us understand your kind better, even as you learn about us. Spirit of the Wolf, this statue is your anchor, this statue is your home within our home. Welcome, and Blessed Be."

As Mariana chants, she builds a cone of power, but this one is not focused on sending out toward a spell; rather it is focused on inviting in an energy. Like a reversed cone, the funnel points directly over the anchor.

She sees the spirit of a wolf coming toward her; it enters the Circle and goes toward the statue. As it does so, she understands that the wolf spirit is a female, and that—for now—she wants to be called Yanaya. The wolf spirit leaps into the cone of power and channels down into the statue. Mariana feels the energy go racing into the statue after the wolf, and she knows that the guardian spirit for her household has chosen to accept her invitation.

After Invoking an Animal Spirit . . .

What do you do with the spirit once it's there?

Well, if it's an animal guardian, you pretty much leave it alone, check on it now and then to see if it wants something, supply it with whatever you promised to give it (for example, we give Krikki new apples every week), and all should go well. Occasionally, if I have a nightmare or get the sense that something is a bit weird, I call Krikki and ask him to have a look to see whether there is anything untoward in the house, and he checks for me. I can sense him lumbering around, keeping an eye out for us.

With an animal guide, you will probably want to meditate frequently, asking for help in learning what lessons you need to learn from it. As with totems, you might want to find jewelry or make a fetish or a medicine or charm bag that matches the energy of the animal spirit guide so you can strengthen your connection with it.

Guided meditations and journeys, divination, and your own inner guidance will help you formulate rituals that will enhance your work with your animal spirit. Rituals set off alarms in the subconscious that a certain pattern of events is to be expected. Even though eclectic magic is a wonderful thing, it's nice to set up a few patterns for yourself. These patterns act much like Pavlov's bells did on his dogs, whetting the subconscious appetite for magical work. By invoking the animal spirit in a ritualistic manner each time you go journeying, you not only pay it respect, you also prepare yourself for the work and lessen your distractions.

In Summation

When invoking spirits, be they animal, human, or from another realm, we must always remember that we are not invoking to control. We must set aside our egos and remember that we share in this Universe with a vast array of entities. When a beneficent astral spirit chooses to work with us, we are the ones who should feel honored. Never abuse your magical powers by attempting to order the spirit around. If you do so, you may run the risk of psychic attack, or you may offend it so that you'll never have another opportunity to work with one of its kind again. Play nice, and you'll likely find yourself with a new and unusual friend.

Part Two

Totem Magic

Quarry mine, blessed am I
in the luck of the chase.
Comes the deer to my singing.

—Navaho Hunting Song

Mystic Totemic Rites:
Totem Magic in Daily Life

Strengthening the Connection with your Totem Spirit

There are times when it feels as if the energy of my totems pulls away. When this happens, I first tune in to see whether it's time for one of my other totems to take precedence for a while. If not, I look for ways to strengthen my connection with my totems.

I've found it handy to keep representations of each of my totems on my altar. Using these figurines, I have a focal point on which to direct my energy when working with them. I have a big candle of a black panther resting near my perfumes for my panther totem, a small green rubber snake that reminds me of my green boa, and a peacock pin for my peacock. Eventually, I will replace all of these items with actual statues. When I want to empower one of my totems, I anoint the power object with an oil I've specifically made for that totem and invoke his or her energy, raising a cone of power and focusing it into myself.

Totem Animal Spell Work during Samhain

The season of Samhain is perhaps one of the best for working with your animal totems because all the spiritual realms are so close to our own, and shape-shifting energy seems to go hand in hand with the transformations taking place that time of year. In my book *Magical Meditations* you will find a totem animal meditation that you can use during Samhain rituals.

Regardless of what kind of ritual you choose to perform for the holiday, you might want to prepare a totem-o'-lantern to use during your meditation. Or you can carve one to use for scrying on Samhain Eve, or just for fun.

Find a good-sized pumpkin that suits your carving. When deciding on size and shape, consider whether or not you are going to carve your whole totem or just the face. Pumpkins are usually inexpensive, so you might want to get a spare in case you make a mistake. Pumpkins make good food for both humans and animals so if you do screw up, you can just bake your mistake with honey and butter, or you can give it to the birds or use it in your compost pile.

Select music and incense that embody your totem's energy. Gather a collection of pictures of your totem and set them around the table on which you are working. If you can find a good documentary about the animal, running the program can add a nice touch to the ritual. If you like, mute the sound and play music instead. Clean out the pumpkin and prepare it for carving.

When ready, cast a Circle and invoke the spirit of your totem. Carve your pumpkin, keeping your focus on it the whole time. It helps if you aren't interrupted, so try to do this when you are alone. It's interesting to notice how deep into trance you can sink while carving a pumpkin and how strong a connection you can forge with your totem during this activity.

Creative Collages for Your Totems

I've also made creative collages for my totems. I usually don't create separate collages for each totem because they work together to make up the whole of my nature, so I make only one collage that contains all the images and essences of all three of my totems.

I am willing to buy magazines for one or two pictures in order to get what I want because it's very difficult to find good pictures of black panthers and green boas. Peacock photographs are much easier to find. You can cast a Circle in which to create and charge your collage if you like, but it isn't necessary. After I've created my collage, I raise energy, charge the collage, and frame it, putting it in a room where I can easily see it so it constantly works on my subconscious, as well as continually working on a magical level. I recycle the rest of the magazines or give them to friends who want to use some of the other pictures for their own collage work.

Magical Chants for Your Totems

Creating magical chants to invoke your totems can increase their influence in your life. It's easy to do, and it takes only a few minutes to come up with a two- or three-line chant. Here are a few examples that I've written, but don't be shy—make up your own based on what you have observed and learned from your totems.

PANTHER

Panther, dark as blackest night,
Bring forth your mystery to my heart,
Strengthen now my will and might,
Let my senses be keen and sharp.

GREEN BOA

Slither serpent, you arboreal dream
Sensuous, creative, with eyes agleam,
Coil round my soul to stay
Help me learn to dance and sway,
Be with me, snake of jungle green,
Graceful, moving soft, unseen.

PEACOCK

Shrill and raucous, feathered bird
Make me be seen, make me heard.
Shine me bright, strengthen me bold
Ancient one, both young and old.

WOLF

Bay to the moon, howl in the night,
Loyal and wise, my teacher so bright.
Feral and wild, run through the trees,
Guide me, Pack Master, help my spirit fly free.

TURTLE

Mother of earth, you are oldest of all,
Guide me to answer when I hear your call.
Slow, strong, steady, graceful and wise,
Let me view the world through your glittering eyes.
Let me swim through the waters in which we evolved,
Gently dig at my problems until they are solved.
Perseverance and patience, your lessons I learn,
To navigate all of life's twists and life's turns.

SQUIRREL

Dart along the fence, then dash up the tree,
Stock away nuts without worry, with ease.
Teach me your love for detail and fun,
Teach me to tease, and teach me to run.
For you are a joker, yet practical too,
Teach me to be merry and thrifty like you.

As I said, it's easy to come up with personalized rhymes and chants for your totems that fit the energy of what you need to learn from them. Try to keep them under eight lines; four or six are easiest to remember. You can create a ritual around your chants, empowering them in Circle. You can sing them under your breath when you need energy reinforcement, or you can use them like a mantra while walking or exercising or just hanging out in the hammock on a warm summer's day.

Dancing Your Totems—Part Two

Once you know what your totem or totems are, you can dance them in ritual. This can be done alone or with others, though I'm going to tell you a story to give you an idea of what can happen when conflicting totems are brought into the same circle.

A friend and I used to dance our totems a lot. Kay, at the time, was dancing Owl and I was focusing on Green Boa. One night we were dancing in Circle and the energy was very high. She started swooping in on me, dive-bombing me in her dance. Owl had really taken hold of her, and Owl was going after the snake, which it saw as dinner. Well, I was dancing with my athame, which represented the fangs of my snake, and Boa truly came in and took over.

I raised the dagger on Kay when she made one particularly close pass at me—snake defending against owl—and suddenly, in some part of my thoughts, I realized that I had pulled a knife on my friend. I immediately put it away, and we actually had quite the laugh over that, but it taught us the power of our totem spirits. Owl goes after Snake for food. Snake naturally defends itself. Kay could not resist the power of the Owl as it sensed Snake energy there, and even though she knew I had a dagger and might be startled, she was still pushed by the nature of Owl to "attack" me. And even though I knew the danger of pulling a knife on someone, my boa reacted and defended itself in the only way it knew how.

As I said before, these spirits are real. Do *not* underestimate the power of working with your totem animals. We are not talking archetypes here in the sense of intellectual constructs or concepts. Be careful, and if you practice totem magic with others, think about the possible consequences that might come about. Self-defense won't hold up in a courtroom when you try to plead that you really didn't mean to take a bite out of your friend's leg, that Rattlesnake was simply defending itself against Horse. Oh yeah, the courts would really go for that one. Think before you dance; think before you invoke.

Dancing your totems can be a powerful way not only to strengthen your connection to them, but to strengthen your connection with your own physical self. Dress appropriately. If your totem is a snake, you might wear a sinuous, slinky outfit. If you have a bird totem, scarves can imitate feathers. If you have a bear totem, then perhaps you will want to wear something with a bit of fur in it. You can also wear a medicine pouch or charm bag around your neck.

You can use makeup for good effect here, so be creative. Paint scales or cat's eyes on your face with eyeliner. Buy or make a mask that fits your totem's energy. Fragrance can play in too; I make oil blends for my totems, and you might want to do the same. Or you may have a perfume or cologne befitting the energy of your totem.

Use mood lighting. Candles or low lights work best. Do be cautious whenever using candles during an ecstatic dancing ritual. Sometimes the energy can get so wild that altars and small tables are knocked over, and you don't want burning wax spreading on your carpet. I try to keep candles up away from where the dancers are dancing. I'm much more likely to use very low-level lights that are not fluorescent. Christmas lights are especially good for this, and the twinkling variety adds a nice Otherworldly–Faerie Realm touch of energy.

When picking your music, try to match the energy to your totem. You may want something ethereal for herons, swans, or doves. Hard rock may work for predators and big cats. Other creatures will call for music like world beat or drumming. If you have several disparate totems present at the ritual, you might want to create a compilation tape or CD so everyone gets a chance to dance to music that fits their animal spirit's nature.

Remember that you are calling in spirits, so err on the side of caution and cast a Circle. Invoke the elements and your totems. Then put on the music and let the energy take over. If you like, you can develop a focus beforehand and direct the energy raised toward that end, or you can channel the energy back into yourself to strengthen your bonds to the animal spirits.

When everyone is tired and the energies have been spent, thank all the spirits and elements and release the Circle. Make sure to eat afterward so you can ground yourself. Spiritual work of this sort takes a lot out of you and can leave you in a state of altered consciousness, which may be fun, but it isn't necessarily safe if you have to drive home.

Mirror Spell for Shape-Shifting

When you decide that you are ready to go deeper into the nature of what it means to connect with your totems, you may want to explore mirror shape-shifting. It can be disconcerting, to say the least, and you must be able to put away any fear of losing yourself in the process. Before you consider this stage, you should prepare yourself in advance:

* You need to know, in your heart, what your totem is. You must know this on a gut level, not just "think" it.

* You should have known about your totem for at least a year, perhaps longer. You should have studied about it so you understand its basic tendencies and nature.

* You should have already danced your totem or drummed it; in other words, you should have approached your totem on a shamanic level frequently for a few months before attempting this.

* You must accept all aspects of your totem, not just the pretty aspects or the nice ones. If you have a totem that eats insects, you need to accept this without being repulsed by it. If your totem rips other animals to shreds for food, again you need to understand and accept on a gut level that this is nature's cycle.

* You need to have done enough trance work to be able to slide into trance easily.

Once you're ready, you will want to perform this ritual either in front of a wall mirror or in front of a bathroom mirror. You will need music that can lull you into a hypnotic state. You will also need two candles in holders that are tall enough so when placed on opposite sides of the mirror, they frame your face with light.

Thoroughly smudge the room where you will be performing this ritual. Cast a Circle and invoke the elements. If you like, call in the god or goddess with whom you are most comfortable working. Light the candles and turn on the music.

Place the candles out of your way, with the flames about the height of your cheekbones. They need to reflect in the mirror. Make certain your hair, or whatever you are wearing, doesn't hang too close to the flame. You don't want to explore dangerous fire magic. Take several slow, deep breaths, exhaling easily and smoothly. Shake your body a little to loosen any kinks. Then lean close to the mirror. When working with bathroom mirrors, you can lean on the counter for balance.

Focus your eyes on a place about half an inch above your head; if you look directly into your own eyes you will develop eyestrain. Begin to breathe slowly at an even pace. Invoke the spirit of your totem animal, through chanting or through summoning it. At the same time, feel your inner connection to the totem spirit as it rises up through you and looks out through your eyes.

Continue to stare at the area above your head, and let your eyes slide a little out of focus. If all goes as planned, within a few minutes you should be able to see your face shift. Don't be surprised if strange faces show up in place of yours. Most likely, if you have warded and protected the area, these will be past-life images coming up from your subconscious. At some point, you should see a glimmer of your totem peeking out from your eyes. It may change the shape of your face a little, it might change your expression, you may see it superimposed on your reflection, you may feel it coiling inside of you, or you may feel it expanding out and stretching as you acknowledge its energy.

When you are ready to stop or if you get too frightened by this exercise, breathe carefully, look away from the mirror and shake your head, then turn on the light, devoke the elements and open the Circle, then smudge the area again. Ground yourself with food and television, different music, or a book.

One of the major drawbacks I found with this mirror work is that I enjoyed the feeling so much I wanted to stay in Circle half the night, watching the changes and shifts, but it's wearing on the body, and I had to force myself to stop after a while.

I did get the creeps a few times. When you're looking in a mirror and somebody else's face is looking back, it's hard not to jump. What helped me overcome this fear was knowing that these were all aspects of myself, of my higher self, and all the beings I have been. After practicing this exercise several times, I got to know and recognize a few of the images. The Mongolian warrior was the most prominent, and I can still feel him inside me: he's still a part of my soul energy, and he comes through at times for me to lean on when I need strength.

Full Moon Totem Dreaming Pillow

If a problem is bothering you, and you think that one of your totems might be able to help, a simple method can help you to work magic in the dream state.

First you will want to make a dreaming pillow, one for each of your totems. When the moon is in the waxing stage, make a pouch of about five by five inches (when finished) of a material that seems appropriate for your totem. For my black panther I'd use black velveteen, for my green boa, I might use a green-and-black-speckled jacquard. Whatever suggests your totem to you will be fine.

Under the full moon, fill each pouch one-third full with cotton batting, then one-third with Dreaming Herbs Mix, and the last third with more cotton. Add a small charm of some sort that is connected to your totem (silver charms are inexpensive and easy to find in the shapes of most animals). Sew the pillow shut, then raise energy and charge in Circle while invoking your totem. Tuck the dreaming pillow in the pillowcase of your top pillow and do not get it wet. This dreaming pillow should last for a year if you anoint it with extra Dream-Walker Oil (or another magical dream oil) every full moon.

DREAMING HERBS MIX

You can use this mixture for herbal dreaming pillows of all kinds, for sachets, and for incense.

> 1 part hops
> 1 part mugwort
> 1 part rose petals
> 1 part lemon balm
> $^1/_2$ part lavender
> $^1/_2$ part chamomile
> 21 drops Dream-Walker Oil

In Circle, blend the herbs with your hands or a mortar and pestle. Add the oil. Raise energy and charge, focusing on invoking a gateway to the Dreamtime, then fill the pillows as directed above.

DREAM-WALKER OIL

Use this oil in dreaming pillows or dab it on your forehead just before going to sleep or whenever you want to reach a deeper state during meditation.

> $^1/_4$ ounce almond oil
> 13 drops lavender oil
> 13 drops chamomile (or lemongrass) oil
> 7 drops jasmine oil
> 7 drops bergamot oil
> 5 drops lemon oil
> 3 drops rosemary (or rose geranium) oil
> A few powdered chamomile flowers
> A chip of moonstone

In Circle, blend the oils. Add a few powdered chamomile flowers and a chip of moonstone. Raise energy and charge, focusing on dreaming magic. Store the mixture in a dark bottle and shake gently before each use.

Full Moon Totem Dreaming Spell

After your dreaming pillow(s) are made and ready, whenever you have a problem and want help from one of your totems, perform the following charm. First, write down your problem on a slip of paper, and tuck it under the dreaming pillow (leave the dreaming pillow inside your pillowcase) in the morning. Let it sit there all day.

That evening, remove the piece of paper, invoke your totem, and ask it to help you find and remember an answer to your problem while you are dreaming. Burn the slip of paper and, when cool, place the ashes in a brazier near your bed.

Go to sleep, focusing on your totem. During the night, you should gain some insight into a solution for, or at least another perspective with which to view, your particular problem.

The next morning be sure to thank your the totem before running off for the day. This spell can be cast whenever you need it. While it is beneficial to make the dreaming pillows during the full moon, you don't have to wait for that phase to take advantage of their magical workings.

A Party of Totems

A fun and interactive way to work with your totem energy in a group setting is to plan a theme party. Have everyone come dressed in the nature of their totem (someone with a cat totem might opt for a long, slinky black dress, while someone with a frog totem might wear a green PVC jumpsuit).

Each person should bring poems or very short tales about their totems, which they wrote by themselves or borrowed from the pages of literature. Have people take turns reading aloud while in character. Panther might use a sensuous voice while Woodpecker might speak in a short, staccato rhythm. You can extend the theme to food, too—predators could bring hearty main dishes, amphibians could bring the munch 'n crunch foods, herbivores could bring the salads, primates could bring fruit salads, and so on.

If you like, there could be a prize for the person who seems to best represent their totem.

Creating Spells with Your Totems

There are many ways that you can magically interact with your totem spirits and create your own spells. You should focus the energy of a spell in accordance with your totem. There's no use asking Panther to help you avoid a fear of flying, nor is there any use asking Rabbit to help you learn how to take charge at the office. Play it by ear, paying attention to the qualities of the particular totem you are working with, and use your correspondences (see Appendix 1: Magical Rites and Correspondences) when you are designing spell work.

Beware the Jabberwock, my son!
The jaws that bite, the claws that snatch!

—Lewis Carroll, "Jabberwocky"

Wolf Wise:
Predators and Protection

The Nature of the Beast: Hunters

It isn't easy to admit that your cute little kitten is an intrepid and ruthless hunter. Or that your puppy is a cousin to the packs of wild dogs and wolves that chase down their prey with precision and efficiency. The truth is, in our society, we have a tendency to avoid the fact that many of us are predators and that we also kill to live. We all kill other living entities for food—vegans and vegetarians kill plants; omnivores kill both plants and animals. Anyone who uses any form of leather or animal by-product lives upon the flesh of others. And this is natural; it's all part of the food chain.

Predators are a necessary part of the ecosystem—too few, and the herds of prey animals increase, resulting in famine and disease. Too many, and they over-hunt, thus starving themselves.

Life and death are shadow sides of existence. If nothing ever died, the world would perish amidst rampant fecundity. Death is part of the natural cycle, and as much as westernized society goes out of its way to portray it as an evil force that snatches us in a malign frenzy of hatred, death is simply the natural end of life.

Now, predators in our society are something quite different from a predator animal spirit. Wanton murderers, especially those like Ted Bundy or Jeffrey Dahmer, are aberrant forces within society; sociopaths have always been with us, but until the modern era, they weren't easily discovered or caught. They are deviant spirits and cannot be equated to the predators in the natural world—the big cats and bears and wolves and sharks that subsist on smaller animals. To destroy life for sport is cruelty at its worst, and I include sport hunters in that category. To hunt for food is one matter, to kill for the love of killing or for trophies is quite another.

A hunter in the natural world seeks food and defends its territory. This comprises both the energy of the hunt and the energy of protection and, when absolutely necessary, the energy of offense. As I watch my cats yowl through the window at the orange kitty who visits our home, I see territorialism in action. This is *their* home, and they are determined to keep out the stranger who might supplant them and take away their food and attention. I wish they wouldn't be so mean, but this is their nature.

When we have predator totems, we find ways to express the instincts of both the hunt and protection. Perhaps we actually hunt for food, like Andrew. Or we might apply the energy in other areas of our life, such as taking on new challenges and persevering till we conquer them, using our questing ability to ferret out information for our work and other projects.

Predator energy involves leadership and strength, being willing to shoulder major decisions that affect others. So too, the king of the jungle must know when to allow a potential meal to walk away. The best leaders rule through encouragement and praise, as well as through discipline. In watching the hierarchy in my feline family, I notice when Pakhit allows the other cats to pick on her and tease her, and when she puts her furry paw down and instills respect with a well-placed swipe.

Spell Work for Predator Totems

When working magic using a hunter's energy, there are several things you should keep in mind.

The nature of this energy is primed for shadow magic, such as hexing, so you must be cautious when approaching it. I have always maintained that there is a time and place for hex work, and we must balance the light with the shadow, but it can be dangerous to dabble in this type of magic before you have a firm grounding with your spell work. Never overestimate your abilities; ego is one of your worst enemies when wielding power of any kind. Ego has been the downfall of many Witches new to the Craft, as well as of some who are more experienced. Having presented my disclaimer here, predator energy can be used for binding spells, for mirror magic, and for exorcising unwanted entities and energies from your life.

Magic using your hunter totem is an excellent choice for focusing on achieving goals and mastering new energies. Primed for the quest, this magic tends to respond to "challenge me" dares. If you are attempting to learn new skills or to master a new discipline and one of your totems is a hunter, creating a spell to merge your goal and your totem energy should produce stronger results.

The territorial instinct can be translated into protection for your house, family, and friends. Think of the dog who guards his house, of the cat who marks her territory, of the bear who chases off any perceived threats to her cubs, of the snake who rattles out a warning that yes, he *will* strike if you come too close. Use the energy of your predator totem to your advantage. Instead of letting restless energy build up, give it focus and make it work for you.

Protection Spell

Having problems with nasty astral entities or with someone bothering you? If you have a predator totem, you can call up that essence to protect you and your home against any psychic onslaught.

Much as the smell of a predator will ward off game, the spirit of a predator totem can ward off negative astral entities. You can also ward off thieves and other social miscreants as long as you remember that no magical protection will help in the mundane world unless you take practical steps to back it up. Lock your doors, don't leave your checkbook unattended, don't walk in dark alleys alone at midnight.

The predatory animal is a hunter, and therefore must have a quarry to chase. When we cast a protection spell calling on a predator's powers, we must find a tangible way that it can accommodate our needs. Therefore, we should turn our fears into gremlins via visualization to give the animal a palpable target.

For this protection spell you will need:

* a white taper candle

* a protection oil

* a protective incense such as frankincense or copal

* a representative image of your totem

* a taper candle to represent your totem

Cast a Circle and invoke the elements. Anoint the white candle with a protection oil. Light the incense. Focus on your totem image and feel the power of the animal rise up within you as you light the totem candle.

Visualize the negative energy that is coming your way as little gremlins and say:

~

Spirit of the (name of animal), within my heart,
Let nothing unwelcome intrude upon my hearth.
Let destruction and anger be kept at bay,
As good fortune comes my way.

~

Light the white candle. Visualize yourself running alongside your animal totem as together you frighten the gremlins and chase them away. You don't want your totem—or you—to eat them up because you don't want that negative energy within you.

When the negative energy has scattered, focus on drawing calm and positive energy your way, and see both your totem and yourself reveling in your new-found peace. Thank your totem spirit and the elements, then open the Circle. Let the white candle burn all the way down.

PROTECTION OIL #5

There are many good protection oils on the market, but should you want to make your own, here is a simple and easy recipe for one. You can use this whenever you feel the need for a little extra magical protection—anoint candles, dreaming pillows, and charms with a few drops.

> $1/4$ ounce almond or olive oil
> 5 drops rosemary or rose geranium oil
> 5 drops lavender oil
> 5 drops lemon oil
> 5 drops cedar oil
> Several cedar needles
> 5 black peppercorns
> A quartz crystal

In Circle, blend the oils. Add a few cedar needles, the black peppercorns, and a quartz crystal. Raise energy and charge, focusing on protective energy. Store the mixture in a dark bottle and shake it before each use.

Hunting Bargains

If you need to buy something important and you don't have much money, rub your checkbook or wallet with Hunting Oil (or any good prosperity oil) before you go out. Focus on your totem's energy filtering into the money holder. See yourself stalking the perfect bargain; visualize yourself finding just what you need at a price you can afford. Then follow your instinct when you go out in search of your prey.

HUNTING OIL

You can use this when you are searching for a specific object or during an actual hunt. If you use it during a hunt, I suggest anointing your weapon with a few drops and asking the Lady of the Hunt to guide you in your quest and to help you painlessly kill your quarry. Remember, the Gods of the Hunt hunt for food, not for sport, so don't expect them to help you under the latter circumstances. They will only trip you up.

> $^1/_4$ ounce almond oil
> 4 drops cedar oil
> 4 drops spruce oil
> 4 drops pine oil
> 4 drops vetiver oil
> 7 drops patchouli oil
> 7 drops violet oil
> 7 drops lemon oil
> Several cedar or spruce needles
> A chip of carnelian or bloodstone

In Circle, blend the oils. Add a few cedar or spruce needles and a chip of carnelian or bloodstone. Raise energy and charge, focusing on the energy of hunting and seeking. Store the mixture in a dark bottle and shake it before each use.

Walkabout Protection Spell

There are times when you will find yourself alone in a potentially dangerous situation with no alternative but to try to get out of it on your own. Your car may have stalled and you need to walk to the nearest service station, or you may have been stranded by a bus that didn't show up. In cases like these, when there are chances of being accosted, you can call on the energy of your totem for extra protection. Sometimes the best defense is a good offense.

Visualize your totem spirit rising up to walk beside you. Ask it to keep alert for danger. See yourself as wearing a headdress with your totem's energy; take on the cloak of Panther or Bear or Tiger. As you walk down the street, feel your stride become firm and silent, visualize your reflexes as ready for action but not tense, take even breaths, and stay calm. Most predators have superior senses, so pay attention to smells, sounds, and movements glimpsed out of the corners of your eyes. Keep your head up and your back straight; do not present yourself as a potential victim, but instead as someone to be avoided.

Leader of the Pack Spell

This spell takes a while to prepare, but it is a long-term one and can be the basis for other empowerment spells. Use it when you need to increase your leadership abilities or when you need to become more aggressive in pursuit of your career. If you have trouble accepting your competitive or assertive nature, you may find this spell helpful. As always, back it up with appropriate action. On the physical level, you can't reinforce a goal you haven't worked toward. This spell is designed to produce enough confidence to spur you on, which will in turn produce even more confidence. You will need a table to work on and the following:

* a red taper candle and candle holder

* a wooden box (preferably oak) about the size of an index-card file box without any paint or markings

* Dragon's Blood ink (you can obtain this through most online or catalog retailers of magical supplies, or through many of your local metaphysical supply stores)

* two paintbrushes

* Leadership Oil (use equal parts of High John the Conqueror Oil and Dragon's Blood Oil in place of this if you can't make the oil blend)

* black acrylic paint

* a small charm, silver or gold, of your predator totem

* superglue or a glue gun

* a picture of yourself that will fit in the box

* Strength and Valor Powder

* a red pouch that you can wear inside your shirt or tuck into your pocket or purse (the pouch should close tightly)

* a small piece of carnelian or ruby

If you have a statue of your totem, set it on the table during this spell; if not, find a picture to set up in Circle with you. Place the red candle in the holder in the center of the table after you have carved the following runes on it:

Y: Algiz, ↑: Tir, and S: Sigel

Cast a Circle so that it encompasses the table you will be working on and invoke the elements. Invoke your totem spirit and welcome it into your ritual. Light the red candle and set it back, away from your working area.

First, paint the box and its lid with a thin layer of the Dragon's Blood ink, both inside and out. Make certain you cover the wood completely. As you paint, focus on infusing the box with strength and vitality, with a form of magical fire. Let the box dry, which shouldn't take long. Use this time to blend the Leadership Oil.

When your box is dry, paint the three runes you carved onto the candle onto the inner bottom of the box with a thin layer of black paint. While waiting for the paint to dry, glue the charm of your totem onto the center of the top of the lid; if the charm is three-dimensional, you can affix it so it is standing on the lid. Then prepare the Strength and Valor Powder while waiting for the paint and glue to dry.

When everything is ready, place your picture of yourself into the bottom of the box. Fill the box with Strength and Valor Powder. Using a soft cloth, oil the inside of the lid with Leadership Oil.

Close the box and raise energy from your totem. Ask to understand and increase your leadership abilities. Ask for help in accepting your assertive nature. Charge the box and all its contents. Then take enough of the powder out of the box to fill the red pouch, adding the piece of carnelian or ruby. Carry the charmed pouch with you, and keep the box on your altar or near your bed. Use the powder when you are doing empowerment spells for yourself.

LEADERSHIP OIL

You can use this oil in spells focused on developing assertive energy, taking charge of a situation, or accepting new responsibilities; it is also helpful when you are applying for jobs of a managerial nature.

> $1/4$ ounce sunflower seed oil or olive oil
> 9 drops Dragon's Blood oil
> 9 drops High John the Conqueror oil
> 9 drops ginger oil
> 9 drops peppermint oil
> A slice of sugared ginger
> A chip of carnelian or garnet

In circle, blend the oils. Add a slice of sugared (candied) ginger and a carnelian or garnet chip. Raise energy and charge, focusing on the energies of leadership and assertiveness. Store the mixture in a dark bottle and shake it before each use.

STRENGTH AND VALOR POWDER

The herbs listed here are connected with the planet Mars and the Sun, the planets that rule our assertive natures. You can use this powder in sachets or sprinkle it in your briefcase (it does have oil in it, so it may stain papers). Or set a little jar of it on your desk. Use dried herbs and leaves and crumble or powder them to measure.

> 1 part basil
> 1 part oak leaves
> 1 part carnation
> 1 part peppermint
> $1/2$ part galangal
> $1/2$ part grains of paradise
> $1/2$ part frankincense
> 9 drops Dragon's Blood oil
> 9 drops High John the Conqueror oil

In Circle, blend the herbs with your hands or using a mortar and pestle. Raise energy and charge, focusing on the qualities of strength, will, radiance, and empowerment. Sprinkle the oils onto the powder of herbs, and again focus energy. Store the powder in a tightly corked dark jar.

Spirit of the (Fill in the Blank) Box Binding Spell

Name your spell after your totem. This spell can help keep unwanted energies away when you know who is causing the problem, but only if you are positive about who is causing you trouble. While the spell won't hurt an accidental recipient (i.e., if you're wrong about who is causing the problem), it might interfere with your friendship with them.

Warning: If you are in a truly dangerous situation or an abusive relationship, you MUST call the police and/or a crisis shelter; magic will not keep you safe when you are facing someone who is abusive. Magic is an enhancement and you MUST rely on practical means first.

For this spell, you will be working on a table and you will need

* a piece of white cardboard, about the size of an index card

* Dragon's Blood ink or red ink

* several pictures of your totem animal that you don't mind cutting up

* glue sticks and a glue gun

* a small box, about the size of the boxes that checks come in (cardboard is fine)

* clear strapping tape

* a black piece of felt, approximately 10 inches square

* Bind Thy Troublemaker Oil (or any good binding oil)

* something that your troublemaker has written on or touched, such as a picture of them or a strand of their hair; if you can't get these items, then work the spell without them

* tobacco

* two red ribbons, each about two yards long

Cast a Circle and invoke the elements. Print the entire name of your troublemaker carefully and correctly on the piece of white cardboard using Dragon's Blood ink or red ink. Set this aside to dry.

Cut out the pictures of your totem animal and glue them into a montage all over the inside and outside of the box and its lid, making sure that the lid still fits (in other words, don't layer too thick). Use the clear strapping tape to cover the collage work on both the box and the lid to be sure they are affixed. Raise the energy of your totem and ask that it infuse the box with its nature.

Now set the black felt on the table and place the white cardboard with the person's name in the center of the black felt square. Put a drop of Bind Thy Troublemaker Oil onto each letter of their name, and with each drop, say:

⌒

I bind thee from ever again harming me in any form or fashion.

⌒

When you are done, place the connector (picture, hair, or other) over the picture and focus on that person; visualize what they have done that has harmed you, be it vicious and untrue gossip about you or actual physical harm done to you. If you don't have a connector, then just do the visualization. Then place the tobacco on top of the connector. Fold the felt into a pouch around the objects, and thoroughly tie it closed with the first red ribbon. Hold the packet and say:

⌒

I invoke thee, great Spirits of the Land,
Bind this person, stay their tongue and hands.
Spirit of the (totem), I call to thee,
Guard, protect, and watch over me.
Keep this troublemaker far at bay
Push them out of my life today.

⌒

Place the charm in the box and put the lid on. Wrap the second red ribbon around the box, and tie it, knotting it thirteen times. Say:

⌒

I free myself from you and all your deeds
As I will, so mote it be!

⌒

Take the box out of your house to a secluded spot; bury it in a hole deep enough where it won't be found. Walk away and don't look back. Have as little as possible to do with the person and don't go courting trouble by bothering them.

BIND THY TROUBLEMAKER OIL

This oil can be used in most binding spells. Avoid applying it to your skin and do not ingest it; this oil can be extremely irritating to the skin and would certainly give you a nasty stomach problem, if not worse.

$1/4$ ounce olive oil
5 drops pepper oil
5 drops peppermint oil
5 drops rosemary oil
5 drops cinnamon oil
5 drops wormwood oil (or rue oil)
5 black peppercorns
A few red pepper flakes
A chip of garnet or carnelian

In Circle, blend the oils. Add the five black peppercorns, a few red pepper flakes, and a chip of garnet or carnelian. Raise energy and charge, focusing on pushing away that which negatively interrupts your life and on binding those things that have malign intentions toward you. Store the mixture in a dark bottle and shake before use.

When the footpads quail at the night-bird's wail,
and black dogs bay at the moon,
Then is the specters' holiday—then is the ghosts'
high noon!

—Sir William Schwenck Gilbert, *Ruddigore*

Free Flight:
Winged Totems and Clear Sight

Birds of a Feather

While crows, ravens, eagles, owls, and hawks are commonly found as totems among the Pagan community, there are a host of other birds, all of which can be totems, and each one possesses some quality that makes it unique, that makes it stand out among its feathered fellows.

The nature of birds is, of course, an avian one. They spend most of their time high off the ground, in treetops, on rooftops, soaring through the sky in a way we can only imagine or glimpse through activities like hang gliding or sky-diving. Even then, we can't really know what it's like to be a bird, to be able to glide above the land, buoyed up by the air currents.

This freedom from being earthbound allows the spirit to soar, indeed to reach for the heavens. But there is the sense that we must be careful. Birds whet our desire to escape the earth's pull, but even they aren't immune to the forces of gravity. They have to rest at some point; their powers of flight are limited, and if they don't heed their limitations, they will fall.

This same lesson is taught to us through legend and lore. Daedalus created wax wings that would carry him and his son Icarus out of Crete, out of reach of their adversary, King Minos. Daedalus warned Icarus to avoid flying too high, for the sun would melt the wax. Yet if they flew too low, moisture would dampen the feathers and cause them to plunge into the sea.

We can look at this as a metaphor for our own lives. By setting our goals too high—flying too high—we can cause our self-destruction. But if we head in the other direction and settle for underachievement—flying too low—we can prevent ourselves from achieving our goals and reaching our destination. Therefore, bird totems teach us to balance our action.

Unfortunately, the lure of freedom and the intoxication of success enticed Icarus into flying higher and higher; his wings melted, and he tumbled into the sea and drowned. Heartbroken, his father buried him on an island that came to bear the name Icaria, and the sea into which Icarus fell became the Icarian Sea. If we do not pay attention to omens, warning signs, and common sense, we too will fail and drown in our own folly.

In our dreams we sometimes find ourselves flying. Through this ability to transcend the physical into the Dreamtime or Otherworld, we are able to spiral into the dizzying heights and terrifying drops that comprise space and time. This allows us, in spirit, to see the Universe as being multidimensional rather than linear, and this gives us a more accurate view of the changeable and mutable natures of reality.

Flying in our dreams may indicate our attempt to metaphorically rise above a situation, to get a bird's-eye view on an issue we are facing. When in flight, a bird can see the overall picture. Here, we work with the energy of objective rather than subjective perception. When we can see an entire situation instead of our singular vantage point, it becomes easier to understand opposing viewpoints. In this manner, we can seek out ways to approach an issue that will be more effective than floundering in our one-sided point of view.

Flying can also represent sexuality, relating to orgasm. When we let go of our conscious minds and give in to orgasm, we soar. In this sense, the energy connected with birds is the energy of release and surrender, teaching us how to let go of our need for control and to accept the flow of energy as it comes to us.

I find it interesting that, even as I write these words, a Steller's jay just showed up on the branches of a fir tree right outside my window. It let out its unearthly shriek, looked at me, and flew away. I've mentioned my squirrel friends who congregate out there, but seldom do birds appear that low on the tree trunks, and I'm going to take that as a sign that I'm on track here.

To continue, by embracing the extended perception that avian energy offers us, we develop the foresight with which to prepare for unexpected situations. When we see a battlefield in its entirety, we know where our vulnerabilities are. When we look at all the possibilities, we can extrapolate the potential results of various actions. We are forearmed and alert, which is much more helpful than walking through life with blinders on.

The energy of winged totems gives us, among other lessons, the ability to alter our perceptions so we can look at life from a macrocosmic perspective.

Spell Work for Winged Totems

Working magic with winged totems can lead to some interesting spells. Owls are heavily connected to magic and wisdom; ravens are affiliated with battle and shadow work, and a number of other birds, including the blackbird, are considered to be aligned with the Faerie Kingdom. Peacocks are universal symbols for magic and language (and in some cultures, they are seen as bearing the evil eye). Hawks are messengers, and eagles represent the Great Spirit. Within the bird kingdom we find the powers of flight (both physical and mental), divine communication with the world of the gods, the pure power of magic, and numerous other energies. Spells for our winged totems should include the encouragement of a macroscopic point of view, the need for release and surrender, the power of thought and will and wisdom, and achievement of attainable goals.

New Moon Divination Spell

Since totem spirits such as the hawk, the owl, or the raven will often bring us messages from the gods, divination seems natural for working with totems of the winged variety. This spell can increase your ability to perceive divine guidance. You will use a table, and you will need:

* a black candle and candle holder

* Witches' Sight Oil or any good psychic oil blend

* your tarot cards or runes

* a mirror

* a feather or other representation (such as a statue, picture, or candle) of your specific totem spirit

This spell is performed on the night before the New Moon. If possible, position your table (it can be small) so you can see the night sky from where you are sitting. Anoint your black candle with the Witches' Sight Oil. Affix the candle into the candleholder and arrange it on the table along with your cards, the mirror, and the feather.

Cast a Circle, invoke the elements and your totem spirit, light the black candle, and settle yourself at the table. Hold the feather or statue, and visualize yourself flying alongside your totem into the dark night. Sense the connection you have to your totem spirit and let it lead you higher and higher. As you spiral into the sky, say:

～

Spirit of my heart, spirit on wings,
Let me hear your wisdom, let me hear you sing,
Open the gates of knowledge, let my sight thrive,
As into the future, together we dive.

～

Let yourself sink deep into the energy of your totem, then replace the feather on the table and take up your cards or runes. Ask whatever question has been on your mind lately and lay out a reading, taking note of any inner prompting that might lead to unusual interpretations of the cards. Jot everything down in a journal.

When you are done with the reading(s), thank the elements and your totem, then open the Circle and ground yourself. Let your candle burn all the way out.

WITCHES' SIGHT OIL

You can use this oil whenever you want a psychic jolt to open up your intuition. It's also good for dream-work magic and astral traveling.

> ¹/₄ ounce almond oil
> 7 drops lavender oil
> 7 drops lemon oil
> 5 drops Dragon's Blood Oil
> 5 drops camphor oil
> 15 drops sage oil
> A pinch of dried lavender flowers
> A chip of moonstone or quartz crystal

In Circle, blend the oils. Add a pinch of dried lavender flowers and a chip of either moonstone or quartz crystal. Raise energy and charge, focusing on increasing psychic awareness. Store the mixture in a dark bottle. Shake before using.

Parking Spell

Find or make a small plastic or clay representation of your bird totem. Empower it like you would a statue or candle for your altar. Hang your creation from the rearview mirror in your car.

Whenever you are headed into a crowded area and really need a parking spot, ask your totem to lead you to an open spot and then follow your instinct as your bird totem astrally flies overhead and sees where the openings are. Just be careful not to slip into trance while you are driving, and always thank the totem by leaving a scattering of seed or bread for birds in your yard or the park.

Glowing Pentacle Ritual

Use this ritual when you want to boost your psychic energy or strengthen your ability to work with magic. It is a long spell and, starting on the full moon, it takes a whole month to complete; try not to miss any days. Do not perform this spell more than once a year; give it time to work. And don't expect overnight results, though anything is possible.

This spell takes considerable preparation. You will be asking quite a bit from your totem, and a strong connection is necessary to heighten your link and boost the amplitude of your personal power. You will need:

* twenty-eight votive candles—fourteen white, fourteen black

* a statue or picture of your totem

* Increasing Power Oil (or High John the Conqueror Oil)

* a ritual chalice that is clear

* Full Moon Water

* New Moon Water

* a large quartz crystal, at least three inches long (quartz amplifies energy)

* Magical Blend Tea

* ritual music that helps you slip into trance

* a mask that represents your totem (you can make or buy this)

Prepare all the candles in advance by carving each one with these runes in this order: ▷; Thurisaz, ⋋; Perdhro, and ᚠ; Fehu.

Each night before starting the ritual, prepare your altar:

* Place your totem statue on your altar.

* Anoint one votive candle with Increasing Power Oil, and place it in a heatproof container next to your chalice. During the waxing to full moon nights, use white candles; during the waning to new moon nights, use black candles.

* Fill your chalice with water and add one fourth cup of moon water—Full Moon Water during the waxing to full moon, and New Moon Water during the waning to new moon. (See appendix 1 for New Moon Water and Full Moon Water.)

* Make a cup of Magical Blend Tea and place it on your altar.

* Set the quartz crystal within easy reach on your altar.

On the evening of the full moon, cast a Circle, invoke the elements and your totem, light a white candle, and turn on the music. Put on your mask and begin to dance your totem. If for some reason you cannot dance your totem, then put on your mask and visualize yourself dancing, moving whatever parts of your body you can move to the music. Build the energy.

When you feel empowered with the energy of your totem, take your place in front of the altar. Remove your mask so you can drink the tea and anoint your forehead with a few drops of moon water. Replace your mask.

Pick up the quartz crystal and tune into its energy; let the crystal's resonance fill your hands. Feel it spreading through your body.

Close your eyes and visualize a glowing pentagram hanging in the air in front of you. See it changing colors: start with red, then move into orange, yellow, green, blue, indigo, and brilliant white. As the pentagram changes color, visualize it moving forward and into your chakras. Red will enter your first chakra, orange your second, yellow your third, green your fourth, blue your fifth, indigo your sixth, and pure white your crown chakra. When the pentagram enters your body, feel its energy move through your kundalini and merge with your own energy. (See appendix 1 for a chakra chart.)

When you have worked your way through the seven colors, drink the chalice of moon water and see yourself sweeping up and into the sky along with your totem; soak in the balanced energies of the moon and the sun. Then remove your mask, thank your totem, and go to sleep for the night. Leave your Circles up and cast a new one each night.

Throughout this month, do not drink alcohol, do not smoke (if at all possible), drink a lot of water, and eat healthy foods. Ground yourself every day with some form of exercise. Avoid too much television, and write down your dreams.

This is a long and complex spell. Magical training doesn't come easy, and if you aren't willing to earn knowledge with your time and labor, you've picked the wrong path.

INCREASING POWER OIL

Use this oil when you need a boost for ritual or spell work. You can also anoint power objects with it and use it as a general amplifier for most spells.

> 1/4 ounce almond oil
> 21 drops Dragon's Blood oil
> 13 drops High John the Conqueror oil
> 13 drops wormwood oil
> 7 drops lemongrass oil
> 7 drops sandalwood oil
> Dragon's Blood resin
> A chip of quartz crystal

In Circle, blend the oils. Add a small chunk of Dragon's Blood resin and a chip of quartz crystal. Raise energy and charge, focusing on increasing the energy of the magic being performed. Store the mixture in dark bottle. Shake before use.

MAGICAL BLEND TEA

This tea can be used before any ritual, and it also makes a good nervine, acting as a mild sedative. Do not boil your water (for any tea), just bring the water to the point of steaming and pour one cup over one tablespoon of tea. Strain and drink.

> 1 cup chamomile
> 1/2 cup lemon balm
> 1/2 cup valerian root
> 1/2 cup kava kava
> 1/2 cup mugwort
> 1 cup peppermint
> 1/2 cup dried lemon peel (organic)

In Circle, mix all the ingredients and steep for ten to fifteen minutes. Raise energy and charge, focusing on opening up the psyche and expanding awareness. Store the tea in a dark bottle, away from light. The taste isn't exactly delightful, so you might want to add a spoon of honey. Do *not* drink this tea if you are pregnant. Mugwort can cause miscarriages.

Suile-na-Greine Ritual

In Gaelic, the eagle was sometimes called the Suile-na-Greine, or the Eye of the Sun. Connected with solar energy in Native American tradition as well as in Celtic, the eagle is an auspicious and noble totem, especially for those who would lead. Along with other birds of prey like the hawk, these soaring wonders rule the skies. A ritual featuring these birds will help us shine and radiate when we are looking to expand our awareness and connection with all life. This ritual should be performed on a sunny, moderately warm day, preferably during the late morning or early afternoon. You will need:

* sunscreen

* Radiance Oil (or a good solar oil)

* a thermos of cold Solar Orange Tea

* one-fourth cup of Sun Water

* a representation of a feathered cloak—this can be a bunch of scarves fastened to the back of your shirt, an actual cloak (though it should not be heavy), or several pieces of sheer, lightweight material that move in the breeze

* a flute (if you play) or a tinkling chain of bells

* a Wind Wand

* an offering of herbs or fruit to leave for the totem spirits

* a snack for after the ritual

Apply sunscreen before leaving your house; with the depletion of the ozone layer, you cannot be too careful, and there is no sense in putting yourself at risk. Take the sunscreen with you in case you need to reapply some later.

Find a place in a park or forest or on someone's private land where you won't be disturbed. Roughly mark out a large circle with eight stones or pieces of wood, and anoint each one with a drop of Radiance Oil.

Set the Solar Orange Tea and Sun Water in the center of the Circle (see appendix 1 for more on Sun Water), along with your cloak and the flute or bells. Using your Wind Wand, cast your Circle and invoke the elements and your totem spirit.

Anoint your forehead with a drop of Radiance Oil, then hold the Sun Water up to the light and say:

~

I call upon the powers of (totem bird) to energize and bless this Sun Water, that it might add radiance and strength to my rites.

~

Add the Sun Water to the tea, hold the tea up to the light, and say:

~

I call upon the powers of (totem bird) to energize and bless this tea, that its energies might infuse me with the will and strength to shine and radiate, to expand my awareness and see what lies ahead, as well as to understand the lessons through which I have just come.

~

Drink most of the tea, then pour the rest on the ground saying:

~

An offering for (totem bird) and for the Mother.

~

Put on your cloak and pick up your flute or bells. Moving deosil (clockwise), walk the inside of the Circle, either shaking the bells or playing a light air on the flute. Visualize yourself stirring up the energies of the wind and sun; they are magnetized by the sound of your music. When you have walked the Circle three times, take your place in the center and sit down.

Close your eyes and visualize your totem spirit soaring overhead. See your spirit rising up to meet and fly with it. Look over the land as you soar past, seeing it from an aerial perspective. Feel the sun on your wings/arms and let it soak into you and energize you, radiating outward down your feathers/fingers. Let the sun recharge and revitalize you.

If you feel like it, stand and begin a totem dance to the music of nature around you. Or, you can just continue drifting in a meditation on the sunlight. When you feel ready to return to earth, bring yourself back into your body.

Make your offerings while in Circle, and then leave them near the bushes for the animals to find. If you bring herbs, make sure they aren't poisonous. Then open the Circle and eat your snack before you go home.

Making a Wind Wand

You can make a wand that embodies the energy of the winds to aid your winged-totem magic. This wand can be used when working with the element of Air, with winged totems, or in magic connected with the intellect, clear sight, divination, and intuition. You will need:

* a branch of wood, about one and a half feet long, from one of the following trees: maple, hazel, mulberry, pecan, linden, banyan, almond, aspen, or pine

* several strips of long, thin, white leather

* feathers of any and all sorts—if they are dyed, find them in colors to match the element of Air—white, yellow, blue, lavender

* glue

* charms representing birds

* quartz chips (the best are those used in quartz chip necklaces; they are easiest to string)

* dental floss or fishing line

* needle and thread

* silver wire

* additional decorative elements, such as bells; a shiny garland in the colors of Air; dried bird's feet (from roadkill) or clean, dry chicken bones; thin strips of sheer chiffon in the colors of Air; lapis lazuli chips

Using the above components, fashion yourself a wand that represents the Wind to you.

Make sure you use glue that dries clear, rather than the kind that dries opaque or cloudy. Ducot Cement is great for attaching gems to wood, but the fumes are nasty and it takes a while to set. I glue leather strips on my wands to provide a firm grip. When wound around the wand in a spiral pattern, silver wire acts as an energy conductor. Creating a wand usually takes more than one sitting. I recommend making your wand under the phase of the waxing moon, during the sunlight and blue sky of the day (if you are lucky enough to live where it doesn't rain all of the time).

After your wand is finished, take it out on a day when the wind is blowing. Hold it up into the air and focus on the winds. Let the elemental spirits know you are there to get their attention. When you feel in communion with the wind, say:

⁓

Wind and gale, storm and mist
Come now, my wand to kiss.
Infuse it with your strength and might,
With your power of thought and flight.
Powers of Air, you mighty winds
To me and mine, your blessing send!

⁓

Keep your wand on an altar with your winged-totem statue, or hang it from a strap. Store it where it can get fresh, circulating air. You may want to recharge it in the winds about once a month or so.

Solar Orange Tea

Solar Orange Tea can be used whenever you want a little extra energy or vitality in your life. It's quite safe and, unless you are allergic to any of the ingredients, you should be able to drink as much as you like.

> 2 tablespoons honey
> 3 cups steaming water
> 2 bags Orange Spice tea
> 1 tablespoon grated orange zest

Stir the honey into the water until it melts and blends in. Pour the water into a sturdy glass jar and add the tea bags and the orange zest. Cap the mixture tightly and put it out in the sunlight for an hour. Strain.

Radiance Oil

This oil is an excellent choice for solar rites and rituals, for adding some oomph to your energy, or for self-esteem and beauty rituals.

> $1/4$ ounce sunflower or olive oil
> 6 drops orange oil
> 6 drops lime oil
> 6 drops frankincense oil
> 4 drops citronella oil
> 4 drops Dragon's Blood oil
> 1 drop cinnamon oil
> A sliver of lime peel or several dried orange blossoms
> A chip of citrine or garnet

In Circle, blend the oils. Add either a sliver of lime peel or a few dried orange blossoms and a chip of citrine or garnet. Raise energy and charge, focusing on invoking the power of the sun and the qualities of radiance and brilliance into the oil. Store the mixture in dark bottle. Shake before use.

Out of the earth
I sing for them
A Horse nation . . .
I sing for them
The animals

—Sing for the Animals (Teton Sioux)

King Stags and Jesters:
Community and Prosperity

From Kings to Jesters

Deep in the forest, the stag raises his head, sporting a full rack, the tines standing in sharp silhouette against the moon. He is king of the forest, an embodiment of the Horned God. Not a hunter himself, the stag is often quarry, but he is still King of the Woodland. Regal, personifying grace, strength, and fluidity, he is the epitome of masculinity.

From Otter, a jester, to Rabbit, sacred to the Great Mother, we encounter a wide range of foraging animal spirits who embody noble, playful, and magical energies. They exemplify teamwork, resiliency, industry, prosperity and abundance, connections with the Faerie Realm and the Otherworld, self-sacrifice, grace, and playfulness.

Deer, squirrels, zebras, moose, porcupines, horses, elephants, antelope, buffalos, primates, whales, salmon, bulls, seals, and sows—all these foragers are targets for predators, yet they are far from timid. Indeed, the drive to survive has forced them to develop keen senses and quick reflexes.

These browsing animals make up the majority of the mammals on this planet, other than human beings. Where predators must, by their nature, be limited in population, those who feast upon the lower end of the food chain can exist in large numbers without endangering the natural balance. Before humans devastated the ecosystem, these animals roamed the plains in vast herds and swam the oceans in thick pods. Imagine looking across to the horizon and seeing thousands of buffalo ranging the prairies.

We can learn a lot from working with these animal spirits, especially about communication and interaction with others. We can learn cooperation, collaboration, how to share, and how to put the good of the many ahead of personal desires. We can learn about the true nature of an extended family. Foraging animals form strong communities and often work together to protect their young against predators. When we have these totems, we can filter their lessons into all aspects of our lives.

Spell Work for Forager Totems

Totems such as the boar, sow, cow, elk, and rabbit are often linked to prosperity and abundance. Cattle and livestock represent wealth—food to eat, with a continuing supply of newborn animals to replace those culled from the herd. The Norse rune Fehu, $\digamma$, from the Elder Futhark, magically symbolizes prosperity and possessions—essentially wealth—while the primary secular translation of the rune was cattle.

Rabbits represent fertility and, therefore, abundance because of their enormous capacity to breed. Elk, while having a number of totemic meanings, ensured game for the hunter and were considered self-sacrificial animals, offering themselves up when petitioned by hungry humans. Game meat was a gift from the gods. Mielikki, my own Lady, protects the wild creatures in her forest, yet she also parcels them out to those who seek her aid when hunting. She is Mistress of the Hunt, and that involves culling the herd so life may continue. The teamwork and community sense among these animals is a prime candidate for our spell workings.

Keep the Luck Flowing Spell

Cast this spell when things are going well in your life and you want to strengthen your current good luck. This spell isn't for times when you are panicked. It is designed to help prevent you from becoming anxious in the first place. You will need:

* a green taper candle

* Luck Oil

* a green altar cloth

* a representative of your totem

* a few coins

* other objects that make you think of prosperity

* a good attitude

Anoint the candle with Luck Oil and set up your altar with the cloth, statue, and candle. Scatter coins and other symbols of abundance around the altar. Cast a Circle, then invoke the elements and your totem. Light the candle.

Visualize your totem as happy and healthy in the middle of a field. You are sitting next to it, slowly brushing your hand over its back. Feel the connection between yourself and your totem spirit and let your energies blend together. Every time you stroke the animal's back, your hand comes away shimmering with light, and you can feel that light soak into your body and aura. The energy is a magnet for abundance, prosperity, and good fortune. Feel that energy well up within you and begin singing this chant, repeating it until the power peaks:

～

Everything in my life works out
more exquisitely than I plan it.

～

When the power peaks, let the energy fly into the Universe to return tenfold. Take three deep breaths, giving thanks for all the blessings you already have in your life now. Thank your totem and the elements, open the Circle, and ground yourself. Let the candle burn all the way out.

LUCK OIL

Prosperity and luck oils abound, and most can be used with a good measure of success. This particular recipe is focused on bringing good fortune into your life. You can rub a few drops on your checkbook and wallet covers, add it to charm bags, or use it on parchment spells that you plan on burning.

> 1/4 ounce almond or olive oil
> 21 drops cedar oil
> 21 drops frankincense oil
> 7 drops nutmeg oil
> 7 drops lotus oil
> 7 drops High John the Conqueror oil
> 7 drops Dragon's Blood oil
> 7 drops sandalwood oil
> A sliver of nutmeg or a whole dried clove
> A chip of peridot or malachite

In Circle, blend the oils well. Add a sliver of nutmeg or a whole dried clove and a chip of peridot or malachite. You can always use quartz crystal chips in place of specific gemstones if you don't have them on hand. Raise energy and charge focusing on prosperity, good fortune, and abundance. Store the mixture in a dark bottle. Shake before use.

The Totem Treasure Box Altar

It's kind of nice to have altar dressings and spell components that you can use and reuse for similarly natured spells. You can make a treasure box to use in a variety of prosperity spells and rituals. Since this is a permanent fixture, you will want to find a box that you really like. I recommend using a wood box because you can carve it or paint runes on it. To set up a treasure box altar, you will need:

* a green taper or votive candle

* a green glass or brass candle holder

* Financial Stability Oil (or a good abundance or prosperity oil)

* prosperity incense (or one geared toward prosperous energy, such as frankincense)

* oven-hardening modeling clay in green, brown, or gold colors

* paint and brushes, a wood burning tool, or carving tools

* a treasure box (try to find one that is at least six by nine inches)

* Abundance Powder

* a quartz crystal point, three inches or longer

* a green or gold cloth

* a bowl of pennies

Cast a Circle and invoke the elements and the spirit of your totem. Carve the following runes on your green candle and set it in the candle holder:

* ᚠ: Fehu represents an increase of wealth and possessions and protection of your valuables; fire in an uncontrollable, primal state is used to propel energy into a spell working.

* ᛒ: Berkana represents growth, abundance, fertility, the Earth Mother, protection, and the culmination or zenith of a situation.

* ᛟ: Othel represents material possessions, protection of possessions, and inheritance (either genetic traits or material inheritance).

Anoint the candle with Financial Stability Oil. Light the candle and incense (if you are allergic to smoke, mix up a bowl of potpourri made out of herbs for prosperity and set it next to your workspace).

Next, fashion the same runes out of the clay; as you mold them, focus on the energy that surrounds each one. Make each rune about $1^1/_2$ to 2 inches long. Bake the clay according to the directions to harden and, if you like, decorate them with gold paint.

While the runes are baking and cooling, paint, carve, or wood burn a representation of your totem on top of the lid of your treasure box. Then paint, carve, or wood burn the same runes on the inner bottom of your treasure box. If you paint, apply a thin coat so it will dry quickly.

Coat your treasure box with Financial Stability Oil and let it soak in (if you painted the runes, do this after the paint dries). Sprinkle a thin layer of Abundance Powder inside the box, then place the crystal and runes inside the box. Now you can arrange your altar; lay out the cloth and place your treasure box on it, then put the bowl of pennies and the candle next to it.

Whenever you need something, write it down on a piece of paper and tuck the note in your treasure box, offering a prayer up to your totem to help you manifest that which you are seeking. Burn the candle for ten minutes while meditating on your need. You can also use your treasure box to create other types of abundance and prosperity spells.

ABUNDANCE POWDER

You can use this powder in sachets, as a powdered incense, or in various spells that call for some sort of prosperity powder. I like this one because it can be made easily with primarily kitchen herbs and a few things from your backyard (depending on where you live).

> 1 part parsley
> 1 part dill
> 1 part basil
> 1 part cedar needles
> 1 part oats
> $1/2$ part patchouli
> $1/2$ part chamomile
> $1/2$ part powdered Dragon's Blood resin
> 21 drops Financial Stability Oil (or other good prosperity oil)
> 21 pennies

In Circle, blend the herbs with your hands. Raise energy and charge, focusing on prosperity and abundance. Add the oil and stir, again with your hands, to mix thoroughly. Add the pennies and store the mixture in a dark jar (leave the pennies in the jar when removing powder for spells).

FINANCIAL STABILITY OIL

This oil is oriented toward stabilizing situations and then infusing them with energy for growth. You can anoint your checkbook the day you make a large deposit; or after you pay off a big bill, you can anoint the zero balance receipt with oil and tuck it with the rest of your bills; things like that.

> 1/2 ounce almond oil
> 8 drops bergamot oil
> 8 drops cedar oil
> 8 drops patchouli oil
> 8 drops nutmeg oil
> 8 drops chamomile oil
> Several cedar needles or chamomile flowers
> A chip of malachite, tigereye, or hematite

In Circle, blend the oils. Add a few cedar needles or chamomile flowers and a chip of malachite, tigereye, or hematite. Raise energy and charge, focusing on stability and security. Store the mixture in a dark bottle. Shake before use.

Sacrifice Spell for a Friend

During the hunt, many native traditions included asking an animal to give up its life so the hunter and his family might live. The elk or deer would often offer itself in a clear shot after the proper prayers were made and offerings given. If you have such a food-providing totem, you can put this energy to good use.

Sometimes we have a friend who desperately needs financial help, but we don't have much to give. We help no one if we get ourselves kicked out of our home because we gave a friend our own rent money so they could pay their bills; this sort of sacrifice only builds resentment. But we can, during those times, perform a spell for our friend that incorporates the energy of self-sacrifice while calling on the Universe, yet which doesn't bankrupt our own checkbooks. For this spell, you will need:

❊ a statue or representation of your totem

❊ Friendship Oil

❊ a green taper candle

* ¼ cup dried marjoram

* a plant pot full of potting soil

* a sweet pea or lavender plant

* Full Moon Water (or bottled water)

* Three four-foot-long ribbons: one each of pink, green, and gold

* whatever gift of money or (if appropriate) food that you can comfortably give to your friend

Cast a Circle and invoke the elements and your totem spirit. Anoint the statue with Friendship Oil and set in the center of your working space. Then carve the following runes onto the candle:

* X: Gebo represents partnership, gifts, and cooperation

* ß: Berkana represents growth, abundance, and fertility

* M: Daeg represents breakthroughs, new directions, increase, and prosperity

Anoint the green candle with Friendship Oil, set it in the holder, and light it. Mix the marjoram, which promotes happiness, with the potting soil in the pot. Focusing on your friend, hold the sweetpea or lavender plant in your hands. Visualize your friend getting everything he or she needs to be happy. Feel your own happiness, knowing that your friend won't be struggling financially. Now pot the plant and water it appropriately.

Tie the three ribbons together at the top and braid them. As you lace them into a braid, repeat the following chant until you are finished braiding:

~

A braid of hope, a braid of love
May blessings shower from above.

~

When you have braided the ribbons, tie off the end, wrap the ribbon around the pot of flowers, and make a big bow. Call upon the spirit of your totem and ask that blessings offer themselves to your friend in need. When you are done, give your gift of cash (anointed with Friendship Oil) or food and the flowers to your friend. Explain that your friend should tend the flowers carefully, that they contain wishes for love and joy.

FRIENDSHIP OIL

You can use this oil in spells that surround friendship issues, whether it be calling for new friends, resolving problems with old friends, helping friends, or just strengthening current relationships.

> 1/2 ounce olive oil
> 7 drops lemon oil
> 7 drops violet oil
> 5 drops rose oil
> 5 drops rosemary oil
> 3 drops cypress oil
> 2 drops clove oil
> A dried rose petal
> A chip of rose quartz or amethyst

In Circle, blend the oils. Add a dried rose petal and a chip of rose quartz or amethyst. Raise energy and charge, focusing on the loving friendships you have and how much you enjoy those caring connections. Store the mixture in a dark bottle. Shake before use.

Running with the Herd—Cooperative Magic

There are times when you will need to be part of a group, when cooperation and compromise are vital for good results. If you have a forager totem, then you can use their energy to focus on the connections between you and others who are working on similar goals or projects.

Part of this process involves setting aside the ego and accepting, at least for this particular issue, the loss of a certain amount of individuality. A group is only as strong as the weakest member belonging to it. When you are working in a collaborative setting, no one person other than the team leader can take precedence over the others. Each person must find the niche that they can best occupy within the overall organization, much like ants or bees in a nest or a hive.

Creating an atmosphere in which all members feel productive and necessary to the whole is far from an easy task; a lot of factors can disrupt the group process, including jealousy, envy, disparate workloads, and favoritism. These dynamics will always be present, even under the best of circumstances, so anything we do to negate their energy is a plus.

While it would be ideal if all members of your project were Witches and could participate in a ritual together to smooth the group's path, this is an unlikely situation. But there are things you can do to foster equanimity and cooperation.

Group Dynamics Sachet

While you obviously can't go to work and light a row of candles on a counter there, you can make up an herbal sachet and tuck it in a corner drawer of your desk if you have one. If you don't have a desk, you can keep the sachet in your purse, your briefcase, or your locker, or you can make a smaller version to wear in your pocket or around your neck and under your shirt or blouse. You will need:

* a pale yellow pouch, five by five inches

* a green fabric paint and a brush

* a charm representing your totem

* Dynamic Cooperation Powder

* five small stones: one each of rose quartz, clear quartz, tigereye, carnelian, and lapis lazuli

* a green ribbon

Cast a Circle, then invoke the elements and your totem spirit. On the front of the yellow pouch, paint these runes with a thin layer of green paint:

* ᚠ: Ansuz represents clear communication, wisdom, and a collaborative focus.

* ᛗ: Mannaz represents cooperation, teamwork, and new projects.

* ᛃ: Jera represents harvesting tangible results and the effective culmination of a project.

While the paint is drying, hold your charm while you explain the nature of your project and the need for group communication and cooperation to your totem spirit and ask for help with magic to smooth your path. Fill the pouch with Dynamic Cooperation Powder and add the charm and the stones. As you add each stone, focus on the following energies:

* rose quartz—peaceful interaction, calm overtones, friendships, and cooperation

* clear quartz—clarity and the ability to discern correct action

* tigereye—stability, security, grounding energy, and manifestation

* carnelian—creativity, passion for work, and inner strength

* lapis lazuli—wisdom, insight, and intuition

Tie the pouch shut with the green ribbon and ask your totem spirit to bless the pouch. Then take the pouch to work or keep it close to you when you go to meetings or other project activities.

DYNAMIC COOPERATION POWDER

You can use this powder in sachets and as an incense when you are looking to calm and promote group dynamics, when you are looking to bring out the best in each person and heighten wisdom and insight.

> 1 part spearmint
> 1 part slippery elm
> 1 part lemon balm
> 1 part lavender
> 1/2 part dried lemon peel
> 1/2 part rosemary
> 1/2 part sage

In Circle, blend the herbs with your hands. Raise energy and charge, focusing on your desire to be part of a peaceful and comfortable working situation with successful group dynamics. Store the mixture in a dark jar.

Garnering Cooperation with Cake

There are times at work when we feel at odds with our coworkers (or a coworker) and want to get things back on the right track. I'm not talking about serious altercations where you need to discuss matters with your supervisor, but about tense times such as a deadline crunch or a holiday overflow of work. During these times, tensions flare, tempers get snarky, and the office becomes a decidedly unfriendly place to be.

Make Honey-Bee-Calm Oatmeal Cake to serve to your coworkers. In the first place, sugar is notorious for calming the nerves when one is overwrought. Second, the very gesture of offering a gift can help resolve tiffs. And third, the magic that you put into this cake, calling on the Spirit of the Bees for help, will filter through all who eat it.

Cast a Circle and invoke the elements and the Spirit of the Bees. When you make your cake, remember these hints:

* Focus your energy on calm, peaceful, and friendly thoughts.

* Think about the good qualities of your coworkers and how much you appreciate them.

* As you add the honey, think about the Spirit of the Bees and how cooperation is part of their nature. Visualize a beehive, where every bee is busy working and helping attend to the needs of the hive, content to be part of the whole. Feel the energy run down your spoon into the batter.

* As you add the spices, focus on the energy of the cinnamon, promoting good feelings; ginger, promoting love; and nutmeg, promoting good fortune.

HONEY-BEE-CALM OATMEAL CAKE

Preheat the oven to 350°F. When you stir, always stir deosil (clockwise).

Cake

> 1 cup quick-cooking oats
> 1¼ cups boiling water
> ½ cup unsalted butter
> ⅔ cup white sugar
> ⅔ cup packed brown sugar
> ½ cup honey
> 2 eggs, at room temperature
> 1 teaspoon cinnamon
> ½ teaspoon ginger
> ½ teaspoon nutmeg
> 1 teaspoon baking soda
> 1 teaspoon salt
> 1¾ cups sifted flour

Topping

> ¾ cup brown sugar
> 1 cup flaked coconut
> ½ cup heavy whipping cream or half-and-half
> ½ cup nuts (optional)

Mix the oats and hot water; let stand for twenty minutes. Set aside. Cream the butter and sugars until fluffy. Add the honey and eggs to the batter and beat well. Sift the spices, baking soda, and salt. Stir into the butter mixture. Add the oatmeal mixture and beat until smooth. Stir in the flour, mixing for about two minutes, until all the flour is incorporated and any lumps are gone. Pour into a greased and floured pan nine by thirteen-inch pan. Bake for thirty to forty minutes. Test for doneness by using a toothpick; when it comes out clean, remove the cake from the oven, cover it with the topping, and return it to the oven and broil for three minutes. Makes eight to twelve servings depending on the serving size.

This recipe comes from my family recipe file by the way, and I've adapted it a bit for use here. When I still ate wheat, I loved making this cake; it was always my favorite. So you're in for a treat here.

*The dream is the small hidden door in the deepest
and most intimate sanctum of the soul, which opens
into that primeval cosmic night that was soul long
before there was a conscious ego and will be soul far
beyond what a conscious ego could ever reach.*

—Carl Jung, "The Meaning of Psychology for Modern Man"

The Slither of Snakes:
Working in the Dreamtime

The Oldest of All

Reptiles and amphibians are among the oldest animals of all. They belong to a time when mammals were but a distant glint on the horizon and thunderous lizards ruled the land; they lived long before whales evolved primitive legs, came ashore, and then returned to the oceans forever.

Reptiles and amphibians have existed for millions of years, and most of this time was spent in Dreamtime. While the seasons changed and the planet evolved, time passed on a grand scale, with occasional interruptions for major climactic events such as volcanic eruptions, floods, and great earthquakes, which shaped the face of the world. For the Dreamtime was, and is, the space of creation, the void where anything can be, where the mutable and ever-changing kaleidoscope of life is laid out, though not in a linear and predestined path. This is the birthplace of fate, where all things are still possible.

Definitions of the Dreamtime depend upon whom you are talking to. Some cultures like the Australian aborigines have legends about this concept, which is part of their creation myth. Most shamanistic cultures, including the Native

Americans, the Mongolian Buryat, and the Hawaiians, have their own interpretations of this etheric space. As Witches, we can visit what we call the Dreamtime or, as we often call it, the Otherworld in our trance states and dream work.

As far as I can tell from my work in this mystical, astrally oriented space, the Dreamtime is a place where our linear views of time do not exist. We can travel back and forth through the years, through space, through other dimensions and realities. When we enter the Dreamtime, we exist in an altered state of perception and consciousness. This occurs most easily when we are asleep and actually dreaming, but it can also take place when we are deep in trance. When we visit the astral planes of the Otherworld during trance, it may seem as if the two worlds—the Dreamtime and "reality"—are superimposed upon one another.

In our humanized perception of time, the world moves along quickly. What happens this morning matters this afternoon, rather than when we live according to the pace of the seasons. We accept our lot rather than creating our own destiny.

In Western culture, we deny the very existence of this creation-void-abyss, preferring instead to view the present and past as immobile and unchanging, the future as unknowable. For most who live in our culture, the past is over and therefore a shadow, the future doesn't exist yet, and the only point of reference is "now." This can, in a sense, be healthy—it forces people to live in the present and to actually *do* something with their lives rather than waiting around for fate to strike in their favor. However, it can also promote a shortsighted perception of life. This live-only-in-the-now attitude can lead to abuse of the environment as we ignore the consequences of our actions, leaving future generations to fend for themselves after we have a big party and waste resources.

When we open our perceptions to include the Dreamtime, we eliminate time barriers, and all time frames become accessible. We see how the past, present, and future interact, how working on the astral level creates change on the physical plane. We can work magic in our past using the Dreamtime to change aspects of our present.

When we work with reptilian and amphibian totems, we naturally gravitate toward the Dreamtime. If we don't consciously realize what we're doing, we lose out on the opportunity for exploration and creation, and we may waste valuable chances to restructure our lives, our very world, through interaction in this space.

Spell Work for Dreamtime Totems

Spell work connected with Dreamtime totems often goes much deeper into the mystical vein than work with other totems. Reptilian magic is heavy medicine. We are not only walking the paths of the Earth, but of the Dreamtime as well, and navigation is much more complicated within the ethereal realms.

The first notion we must dispel regarding working with Dreamtime magic is that this work is simply a change of consciousness or a change of perception. We are not dabbling in theory here, but with an energy space that can alter reality, that can shift the nature of events. In other words, we aren't in Kansas anymore Toto, and we aren't intellectualizing hypothetical concepts. We are working with very real energies in a place of very real power.

The second block we must overcome is the idea that, because we don't belong to a certain native or aboriginal ethnicity or culture, we don't have the right to work with certain forces. The Dreamtime existed long before humankind, and as we evolved and took form on this planet, we were all connected to it.

Conversely, I've known several African-American and Chinese-American Witches who met with skepticism when they expressed an interest in Norse and Celtic belief systems. They were questioned as to why they would want to work with these deities, spirits, and magical systems when their ethnic backgrounds lean in a different direction.

I continue to maintain: As long as the seeker is of true heart and listens to the gods, as long as they don't attempt to shortcut their training, then their work should be not be denied due to ethnic or cultural background. With the nature of reincarnation, who's to say we aren't coming home to a belief system that we worked with in a prior life cycle?

No matter what it is called, the different visions of the Dreamtime all refer to the same place. Regardless of heritage, if you are a serious practitioner of magic, you have the right to explore your links with this interdimensional space. If you are working from a Celtic background, you may venture into it with differing terms and methods than someone who is of Hawaiian background, but you are still exploring the same basic energy.

Dreamtime magic focuses on one's connections with the Otherworld, and it tends to be aimed toward intangible directions, such as increasing magical abilities, dream work, astral projection, heightened awareness, or breaking through illusion. Because reptiles are cold-blooded and must frequent warm places to keep active, the magic tends to be solar rather than lunar focused.

As we delve into this Otherworld-oriented energy, most of the spells will be visualizations, meditations, dance work, or other experientially based magical workings.

Thunder Lizard's Dance of the Kings—Empowerment Spell

This spell is focused through dancing and an environment designed to lead you into an altered state of consciousness. If you cannot dance due to physical limitations, you can use this as a meditation. The spell is focused on helping you find that internal sense of empowerment that allows you to feel confident and in control your life. You will need:

* a gold candle

* Conquer Your Fears Oil (or you may use either High John the Conqueror oil or Dragon's Blood oil)

* Empowerment Tea

* Chocolate Furnace Drops (optional)

* incense, either gum mastic, copal, or myrrh

* music with a heavy, steady beat (I recommend Gabrielle Roth's *Trance* or *Bones* or a drumming tape)

Cast a Circle and invoke the elements. Invoke your totem spirit and the Spirit of the Dinosaur.

Carve the gold candle with the following runes:

* ▷: Thurisaz represents protection, breakthrough, and the hammer of Thor

* ≲: Sigel represents the Sun, victory, power, strength, health, and vitality

* ↑: Tir represents leadership, success, virility, and passion

Anoint the candle with Conquer Your Fears Oil, set it in a candle holder, and place it on your altar, along with Empowerment Tea and Chocolate Furnace Drops. Light the candle and incense.

Drink one cup of Empowerment Tea and feel the energy of the herbs racing through your bloodstream. Take three deep breaths and close your eyes. Lower yourself into trance and breathe slowly and rhythmically. Call upon your totem. When you can see or feel it, ask it to lead you through the Dreamtime to the time of the dinosaurs. Follow it through the void until you can see yourself wandering through a landscape.

The world you are now in is filled with dinosaurs, huge creatures that roamed the world, conquering their realm during the time slated to be theirs. Pick one dinosaur to follow. Watch it run, thundering across the plains. Visualize yourself as the dinosaur; imagine how it must have been to be such a huge creature, one of the kings of the land.

Stand and dance the Spirit of the Dinosaur. Feel the strength from its spirit flowing into you, and see your own totem standing next to it, a descendent from these creatures of long ago. Dance the connection between Dinosaur and your own totem—for many theories indicate that they were linked.

Let the sheer power of the spirit's size and strength enter your psyche and race through your body as you cross through the Dreamtime to meet this denizen from ages long gone. When you feel that you have captured some of Dinosaur's strength and power, then slowly lower yourself to the floor or a sofa and stretch out. Let your mind drift out of prehistory and enter the Dreamtime. Watch, but do not analyze, any images that come your way.

Now ask your personal totem to appear before you. When it arrives, thank it for helping you and ask whether it has any advice or requests to make of you. Listen for its answer. After you have finished talking to it, then ask your totem to lead you back to your own time/space/body. When you are ready, take three deep breaths and open your eyes.

Drink another cup of Empowerment Tea and eat something—the Chocolate Furnace Drops will replenish energy and protein, unless you have a medical condition that would prevent consuming them. Other choices are cheese and fruit; crackers, peanut butter, and jam; or smoked salmon, tomatoes, and cheese.

CONQUER YOUR FEARS OIL

This oil is good for bracing your latent courage and bravery. You can use it in a variety of empowerment or self-confidence spells.

> 1/4 ounce sunflower or almond oil
> 9 drops Dragon's Blood oil
> 9 drops High John the Conqueror oil
> 9 drops orange oil
> 9 drops lime oil
> 9 drops frankincense oil
> 9 drops carnation oil
> Several grains frankincense resin
> A chip of citrine or carnelian

In Circle, blend the oils. Add a few grains of frankincense resin and a chip of citrine or carnelian. Raise energy and charge, focusing on the qualities of empowerment, personal success, strength, and victory. Store the mixture in a dark bottle. Shake before use.

Empowerment Tea

You can drink this tea anytime you need extra energy or a boost of vitality. Make sure all the herbs are clean and organic to avoid pesticide residue.

> 2 parts black tea
> 1 part orange blossoms
> 1 part dried lime zest
> $1/4$ part dried ginger, powdered
> $1/4$ part cinnamon, powdered

In Circle, blend all the ingredients. Raise energy and charge, focusing on vitality and strength. Pour one cup of steaming (not quite boiling) water over one table-spoon tea. Steep ten minutes, strain, and serve. Store the mixture in a dark jar.

Chocolate Furnace Drops

These chocolates are a no-bake mixture designed to give you a boost in carbohydrates and protein. They also taste really good. When you make them, do so in Circle, always stir deosil, and focus on the energy you want to instill in them—in this case, stamina, strength, and clarity of mind.

> $1/4$ cup butter
> 2 cups sugar
> $1/2$ cup evaporated milk
> $1/2$ cup baking cocoa
> 1 teaspoon vanilla
> $1/2$ cup peanut butter
> 2 cups oats
> $1/2$ cup raisins
> $1/2$ cup flaked coconut
> $1/2$ cup chopped walnuts or almonds

Mix the butter, sugar, milk, and cocoa in a heavy saucepan. Bring to medium-high heat, constantly stirring with a wire whip. Boil for exactly one minute, stirring to avoid burning. Remove from the heat and add the vanilla and peanut butter. Stir until the peanut butter is melted, then add the oats, raisins, coconut, and nuts. Stir well. Drop by spoonfuls onto a lightly greased cookie sheet or waxed or parchment paper. Cool until hardened. The drops may be stored in a tightly closed container or in the refrigerator. Makes three dozen cookie drops.

Shedding Old Layers Ritual

This spell is especially good for people with snake totems, although it could be adapted for those working with insect totems like the caterpillar or butterfly—all totems that make physical transformations within one life cycle. You will need:

* red and gold or green and gold cloth

* images representing energies you want to shed and to gain

* strings of semiprecious stones

* music that fits the mood

* Transformation Oil, either Mental or Physical

* three candles—one white, one black, one red—and candle holders

* copal or sandalwood incense

* a piece of paper, a quill, and Dragon's Blood ink (or red ink if you can't find the Dragon's Blood ink)

* a piece of black felt, approximately ten by ten inches

* a figurine to represent yourself (small enough to fit inside the snake skin comfortably)

* a shed snake skin from a snake at least an inch in diameter (ask for them at pet stores or from friends who keep snakes)

* a red ribbon, twelve inches long

* two large, green plant leaves—from a maple or ti tree, or some other big-leafed plant or tree

Set up your altar with a red and gold or green and gold cloth. Decorate your altar with images of snakes, of yourself as you are, and of energies you want to incorporate into your life—a collage would be an easy way to do this. Drape strings of pearls, garnets, peridot, moonstones, or quartz crystals around the altar if you have them. In other words, make the altar opulent and beautiful.

Cast a Circle, call the elements, and invoke Snake. Turn on the music. Anoint your forehead with Transformation Oil. Carve the candles thusly:

* On the white candle, carve the rune ᚱ: Raido represents movement, and the removal of stagnation from a situation.

* On the black candle, carve the rune ᛈ: Perdhro represents spiritual evolution, the removal of obstacles, and hidden secrets coming to light.

* On the red candle, carve the rune ᛞ: Daeg represents breakthroughs, growth, expansion, and major turning points in life.

Set the candles into holders and place them on your altar. Light the white candle and the incense.

Using the quill and ink, write on the paper several things that you'd like to transform in yourself. Be honest here. Can you see these things actually happening, or are they pipe dreams? Make certain that they have to do with your body or mind, and not with your environment. When you have recorded your aspirations, apply a drop of Transformation Oil to each "transformational wish" and let the paper dry for a moment. Then burn the paper in a stainless steel bowl or in your fireplace, where you can easily gather up the cooled ashes.

Lay out the black felt and sprinkle the cooled ashes on it. Anoint the figure of yourself with Transformation Oil and raise energy, focusing on what you would like to see transform in your life. Charge the figurine and bless it as a representative of yourself. Very carefully, slide the snake skin over the figurine so it is encased within the skin. If there is leftover skin on the top or bottom, you may fold it over or cut it so there's only about two inches left on each end. Use a few drops of wax from the white candle to seal the ends of the skin so the figurine is entirely sealed within the snake skin.

Rest the figurine on the felt and carefully roll up the felt, with the ends of the material tucked in. Tie the packet firmly with the red ribbon. Place the packet on your altar on one leaf and cover it with the other leaf.

Light the black candle and invoke the Spirit of the Snake (the following is a suggestion, adapt it to your own particular needs):

⌒

Spirit of the Snake, Spirit of All Serpents, I call you forth from the Dreamtime where all reptiles are born and where all reptiles dream. Hear me, my totem, hear me, my animal spirit. I call upon you, you who transform and transmute yourself. Show me how to shed my old skin, show me how to shed the past and come into the present, shining. Show me how to lose the old chains that drag me down as I seek to transform my life, my self.

Spirit of the Snake, come into my body, come into my mind and soul and lead me into the Dreamtime where I may do my work.

⌒

Visualize your totem coiling around you and dragging you with it into the Dreamtime. Let yourself slide into trance as you enter the Dreamtime. Go deeper within; let your mind sink in the energy of the magical working. If you are so moved, you may get up and dance Snake, but you can do this all within trance and meditation if you like.

Listen for guidance. Take note of what you see. Do not argue, simply observe and feel. When you are fully immersed in the energy, begin to channel it between your hands (raise energy) and focus it toward the cocooned figurine of yourself. Let the energy radiate and charge the package and visualize a snake starting to struggle as it tries to free itself from its skin.

Now light the red candle and slowly remove the packet from between the leaves. Keeping the image of the snake shedding its skin in your thoughts, open the felt package and unroll it. Pick up the snake skin–encased figurine and slowly work the skin down from the head. Feel yourself beginning to shed the old layers you've wanted to get rid of—don't be surprised if there is some pain involved (this will most likely be emotional unless you are in a deep empathetic trance). Growing pains are not uncommon on a spiritual level. When you have reached the figure's feet, pull the snake skin off and light it on fire in the red candle's flame, then drop the skin in a stainless steel bowl to burn. Polish the figurine of yourself with a clean cloth and, holding it, drift deeper into the Dreamtime.

See Snake in her new skin, slithering, coiling, dancing the dance of the ages. Join her, in either spirit or body, and let yourself move to the music, free of the old energies that kept you bound down. Dance a dance of freedom, either on the etheric dreaming level or with your body.

When you are ready to return, ask Snake to guide you back to your own space and body and thank her for her help. Take three deep breaths as you slide out of the Dreamtime, open your eyes, and ground yourself. You will want to eat and drink something to fully connect with your body. Let the candles burn out. Keep the figurine on an altar or near your bed.

TRANSFORMATION OIL: MENTAL

This oil blend is based on oils that have a connection to the element Air—a changing, mutable force. If you are seeking transformation on the physical level, use the physical blend listed below. This one is good for changing perception, altering focus, moving blocks to creativity, and so on.

> 1/4 ounce almond oil
> 5 drops bergamot oil
> 5 drops camphor oil
> 5 drops peppermint oil
> 5 drops lemongrass oil
> A dried peppermint leaf
> A chip of clear quartz or aquamarine

In Circle, blend the oils. Add a dried peppermint leaf and a chip of clear quartz or aquamarine. Raise energy and charge, focusing on the mutable energy of Air and how it relates to the thought processes. Store the mixture in a dark bottle. Shake before use.

Transformation Oil: Physical

This oil blend is based on oils that have a connection to the element Fire—a force that creates physical transformation. If you are seeking transformation on the intellectual level, use the mental blend listed above. This one is good for changing body shape and health, for altering one's aura in the lower chakras, for breaking bad habits, and for instilling good ones.

> $1/4$ ounce olive oil
> 5 drops witch hazel oil
> 5 drops carnation oil
> 5 drops frankincense oil
> 5 drops ginger oil
> A dried carnation petal
> A chip of citrine, garnet, or carnelian

In Circle, blend the oils. Add a dried carnation petal and a chip of citrine, garnet, or carnelian. Raise energy and charge, focusing on the mutable energy of Fire and how it relates to the physical form. Store the mixture in a dark bottle. Shake before use.

Breaking Illusion

One of the advantages of possessing a reptile totem is that you will eventually be able to see beyond the illusions that others put up to lead you astray. When you feel that you are being deceived, you might want to use simple trance work to determine whether or not you are correct. This requires several abilities, however. You must be able to:

* sustain a deep trance on your own, which usually means several years of practice

* set your ego and fear aside so you can listen objectively to your intuition

* avoid holding a grudge or feeling envy against this person so you don't taint your results

Divination for hidden secrets generally works best under a new moon, so if you can, wait until the waning to new phase of the moon. Several stones make excellent aids for divination of this sort: obsidian and clear quartz are two of the best. If you are working with rough obsidian be careful; it's razor sharp and can lacerate your hand in the blink of an eye.

Enhance your divination and trance work by drinking an herbal tincture or one of the following herbal teas (yes, the first two taste nasty, but they work): valerian, mugwort, or chamomile. If you are pregnant, do not drink mugwort tea.

Incense can offer additional support. Gum mastic is one of the best for shooting you out into the ether, so to speak. Copal is another good choice.

Music can provide a good background for trance work, but try not to use something that might subconsciously influence your results. You can use peaceful, etheric music or you can go with a more forceful hypnotic beat, whatever works best for you. Avoid music with lyrics.

You do not have to cast a Circle, but throughout this book I've indicated that when working with Spirits, casting a Circle increases your safety. You will be attempting to work in the Dreamtime, and this means there will be other energies and beings out there around you. I advise that you do cast a Circle if possible.

Ask your totem to lead you into the Dreamtime. Let yourself sink into trance and follow your totem spirit until it tells you that you are in the Dreamtime space.

From there, call upon the person you are worried about. Call them psychically to join you. Ask them what their intentions are. Listen to them. From this space, it's difficult for someone connected with the physical world to lie (though not impossible). Ask your totem what it thinks about the person and also listen to your gut instinct—remember, your intuition is not what your heart or head tells you because heart and head can both lie. Intuition is a little voice in your gut that says, "I know . . ."

When you are done talking with the person, thank them and ask that they be escorted back out of the Dreamtime. Then have your totem bring you back to your own space/body. You should have some better insights to go on now and, if you have ascertained that the person is trying to deceive you, you can now decide what you should do next.

That dolphin-torn, that gong-tormented sea.

—William Butler Yeats, "Byzantium"

Afterword

Well, the end of another book, and frankly, what it all comes down to is that you have to make your own way, though you may use bits and pieces of my work to help you navigate the stormy seas of your own spiritual quest. For all quests have stormy seas, and all journeys are remembered not for the ending, but for the adventures. That's what makes them worth telling.

Totem magic is as ancient as mankind and, in its most simplistic form, it is a primal connection between animal and person, between human and the wild. We are beasts, you know, beasts risen from the savannas and jungles and forests. We have come down from the trees and up out of the water, but you can never, ever fully remove the feral nature from our psyches. By connecting with our totem spirits, we can express ourselves and link with other creatures on this planet. And if we ever needed those understanding links, it's now.

The list of endangered creatures grows every day. The list of the extinct—a roll call of the dead for species as a whole—grows longer every year. We can't afford to support politicians who won't protect the environment. We can't afford to support corporations who put profit over ecological concerns. Because we are part of the environment, we are part of the ecosystem. What destroys it, destroys us. We are destroying ourselves, and we are taking the majority of species on this planet down with us. Unfortunately, when a single mother has three children to feed, she's not likely to think about the dying tigers in India, but rather of where she's going to get the money to put food on her table. I fully understand this, and yet—at the same time—this narrow-focused attitude may signify the death of our species.

I want you to do something. Take part in the next election after you read this book (whenever that may be). And in the elections after that. Make your concerns known to your representatives and senators. Vote. Get involved with an organization that mirrors your own feelings toward the environment and animals—even if only through a five-dollar donation or one hour of time spent passing out pamphlets.

If we don't all do our part, then books like this will be useless because we will have killed off the species that we were trying to connect with on a spiritual level. So I'm asking you . . . no, begging you. If I've made any impression on you, in any positive way, please become proactive. Our animal companions can't do it for themselves—it's up to us.

Anyway, I hope that you've enjoyed this book and that it has offered you a different and interesting glance into the world of working with animal totems, spirits, and guides. I'll see you in the next book. Until then, may you always find your way.

Bright Blessings,

—the Painted Panther
Yasmine Galenorn

Magical Rites and Correspondences

Circle Casting and Invoking the Elements

I thoroughly cover casting a Circle (an area of sacred space) in my book *Embracing the Moon*, but I will discuss the rudimentary concepts here.

The idea behind casting a Circle is to create a sacred space where you can practice your magical workings. When you cast a Circle, you create a space charged with magic that is conducive to spellcraft and ritual. There are many ways to cast a Circle; you should experiment to find which way works best for you. You might find that you vary the way you cast your Circle each time you enter ritual. It is a good idea to clean your physical space before you enter into magical practice: sweep, clear out cobwebs, clean up clutter. This will help prevent too much chaotic magic from filtering into your space.

The simplest and most common method of casting a Circle uses a wand, an athame, a crystal, or your hand, through which you will direct energy. Stand in the center of the room, and ground yourself. Raise energy through your body and focus it into your hand, or into a tool if you are using one. Channel the energy out of the tool or your hand to create a line of directed force as you slowly turn deosil (clockwise) in a circle, keeping your concentration focused.

You can add chants, you can create an invocation, or you can cast the Circle in silence. I usually cast my Circles thrice: once in the name of the Young Lord and the Maiden, once in the name of the Father and the Mother, and once in the name of the Sage and the Crone. When you open the Circle, you can use a broom or your hand to sweep the energy away.

Most Witches and Pagans invoke the four elements after they cast the Circle. Together, these elements (Earth, Air, Fire, and Water) create a balance, and when added together they comprise all life. When we invoke Earth, we invoke the essence of stability, manifestation, abundance, solidity, prosperity, and the physical realm. With Air, we invoke intellect, insight, clarity, and new beginnings. Fire brings us transformation, healing, passion, creativity, and sensuality. With Water, we find emotion, the psyche's hidden depths, introspection, and the ability to adapt.

Elemental Correspondence Tables

The Element of Air

QUALITY	CORRESPONDENCE
Sabbats	Imbolc, Ostara
Direction	East
Realms	The mind—all mental, intellectual, and some psychic work; knowledge; abstract thought; theory; mountaintops; prairie open to the wind; wind; breath; clouds; vapor and mist; storms; purification; removal of stagnation; new beginnings; change
Time	Dawn
Season	Spring
Colors	White, yellow, lavender, pale blue, gray
Zodiac signs	Gemini, Libra, Aquarius
Tools	Censer, incense, athame, sword
Oils	Frankincense, violet, lavender, lemon, rosemary
Faeries	Sylphs
Animals	All birds
Goddesses	Aradia, Arianrhod, Nuit, Urania, Athena
Gods	Mercury, Hermes, Shu, Thoth, Khephera

The Element of Fire

QUALITY	CORRESPONDENCE
Sabbats	Beltane, Litha
Direction	South
Realms	Creativity; passion; energy; blood; healing; destruction; temper; faerie fire, phosphorescence and will o' the wisps; volcanoes; flame; lava; bonfires; deserts; sun
Time	Noon
Season	Summer
Colors	Red, orange, gold, crimson, peridot, white
Zodiac signs	Leo, Aries, Sagittarius
Tools	Wand, candle
Oils	Lime, orange, neroli, citronella
Faeries	Flame Dancers, Phoenix
Animals	Salamander, snake, lizard
Goddesses	Pele, Freyja, Vesta, Hestia, Brighid
Gods	Vulcan, Horus, Ra, Agni, Hephaestus

The Element of Water

QUALITY	CORRESPONDENCE
Sabbats	Lughnasadh, Mabon
Direction	West
Realms	Emotions; feelings; love; sorrow; intuition; the subconscious and unconscious minds; the womb; fertility; menstruation; cleansing; purification; oceans; lakes; tide pools; rain; springs and wells
Time	Afternoon
Season	Autumn
Colors	Blue, blue gray, aquamarine, lavender, white, gray, indigo, royal purple
Zodiac signs	Pisces, Scorpio, Cancer
Tools	Chalice, cauldron
Oils	Lemon, lily of the valley, camphor
Faeries	Naiads, Undines, Sirens
Animals	All fish and marine life
Goddesses	Aphrodite, Isis, Mari, Tiamat, Vellamo, Ran, Kupala
Gods	Ahto, Osiris, Manannan, Neptune, Poseidon, Varuna

The Element of Earth

QUALITY	CORRESPONDENCE
Sabbats	Samhain, Yule
Direction	North
Realms	The body; growth; nature; sustenance; material gain; prosperity; money; death; caverns; fields; meadows; plants; trees; animals; rocks; crystals; manifestation; materialization
Time	Midnight
Season	Winter
Colors	Black, brown, green, gold, mustard
Zodiac signs	Capricorn, Taurus, Virgo
Tools	Pentacle
Oils	Pine, cypress, cedar, sage, vetiver
Faeries	Paras, Kobolds, Dwarves
Animals	All four-footed animals
Goddesses	Ceres, Demeter, Gaia, Persephone, Kore, Rhea, Epona, Cerridwen, Mielikki
Gods	Cernunnos, Herne, Dionysus, Marduk, Pan, Tammuz, Attis, Thor, Tapio

Simple Circle Casting and Invocation of the Elements

In the center of your ritual space, stand with your dagger (or tool of choice). Focus on drawing the energy through you and directing it into your blade. Circle slowly from north, deosil (clockwise), three times. Say:

～

I cast this Circle once in the name of the Young Lord and the Maiden.
I cast this Circle twice in the name of the Father and the Mother.
I cast this Circle thrice in the name of the Sage and the Crone.

～

Turn to the north, and say:

～

I invoke thee, Spirits of Earth, you who are bone and stone and crystal, you who are rock and tree and branch and leaf. I invoke thee, you who are deepest caverns to the highest mountaintops. Come to me and bring with you your stability, your manifestation, your abundance and prosperity. Come to these rites, Spirits of Earth. Welcome and Blessed Be.

～

Turn to the east, and say:

～

I invoke thee, Spirits of Wind, you who are the chill breeze, you who are mist and fog and vapor and the gale of the hurricane. I invoke thee, you who are the rising winds and the gentle calm. Come to me and bring with you your keen insight and clarity of mind, sweep through and remove stagnation and bring new beginnings. Come to these rites, Spirits of Wind. Welcome and Blessed Be.

～

Turn to the south, and say:

~

I invoke thee, Spirits of Flame, you who are the crackling bonfire, you who are warmth of the hearth, the golden glow of the sun through the forest at midday. I invoke thee, you who are the glowing lava and the heat of the desert sands. Come to me and bring with you your passion and creativity, your healing and transformation. Come to these rites, Spirits of Flame. Welcome and Blessed Be.

~

Turn to the west, and say:

~

I invoke thee, Spirits of Water, you who are the raging river, you who are the crashing ocean breakers and the still pool of the grotto. I invoke thee, you who are the tears of our body, the rain kissing our brow. Come to me and bring with you joy and sorrow, laughter and tears, peace and enthusiasm. Lead me into the hidden depths of my psyche and guide the way into my heart. Come to these rites, Spirits of Water. Welcome and Blessed Be.

~

Devoking Elements and Opening the Circle

When the ritual is over, you will probably want to devoke the elements and open the Circle. This will open the energy pathways. Occasionally I leave a Circle intact, to settle into the walls of the house.

Turn to the west, and say:

~

Spirits of the Water, Spirits of the Ocean, thank you for attending our Circle. Go if you must, stay if you will. Hail and farewell.

~

Turn to the south, and say:

∽

Spirits of Flame, Spirits of Fire, thank you for attending our Circle.
Go if you must, stay if you will. Hail and Farewell.

∽

Turn to the east, and say:

∽

Spirits of Wind, Spirits of Air, thank you for attending our Circle.
Go if you must, stay if you will. Hail and Farewell.

∽

Turn to the north, and say:

∽

Spirits of Earth, Spirits of the Mountains, thank you for attending our Circle.
Go if you must, stay if you will. Hail and Farewell.

∽

Take your broom, or use your hand, and slowly turn widdershins (counterclockwise) while envisioning the ring of energy opening. If you cast the Circle thrice, then devoke it with three turns; if you cast it once, then devoke it with one turn. Say:

∽

This Circle is open but unbroken.
Merry Meet, Merry Part, and Merry Meet again!

∽

Raising Energy and Charging Objects

While I give a full description of how to raise energy in *Embracing the Moon*, here is a brief overview. The energy we call "magic" is all around us; it exists as auras around everything in the Universe. We can draw upon this energy in our spell work; indeed, it's what makes our spells actually work.

We can focus this energy into an object or toward a desired end by concentrating and building a charge between our hands, then aiming that charge toward our goal. The easiest way to begin experimenting with this is by rubbing your hands together, then slowly drawing them apart. When you feel a magnetic resonance, you are actually feeling magic—energy that you can use. By practicing this on a regular basis and increasing the amount of energy you are able to draw between your hands, you will increase the power of your spell work.

Invoking and Devoking Pentagrams

I discuss this fully in *Embracing the Moon*, but here is a recap. A pentagram is a five-pointed star, with a circle drawn around it. The single point traditionally points up. This an ancient symbol, and it is not to be used or worn lightly—it is a symbol of protection and power, and in my opinion, those who have not earned it through study and practice shouldn't be wearing it. It is a religious symbol, as much as the cross is, and I would never wear the symbol of a religion of which I am not a practitioner.

Invoking pentagrams bring energy in, devoking pentagrams banish or dismiss energy. I use a different devoking pentagram than many Witches because it makes sense to me to devoke in the opposite pattern from the direction of invocation. I present both versions here, and you may choose which works best for you. Arrows show the direction in which you draw the pentagram (with either your hand, an athame, or another magical object).

Invoking Pentagram

Devoking Pentagram (mine)

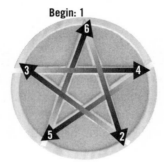

Devoking Pentagram (traditional)

Smudging

Smudging is the act of using smoke to cleanse the energies and auras of things and people. You can use either a stick of incense, some granular incense on charcoal designed for this purpose, or a smudge stick (usually a bundle of sage, or sage and lavender, or sweetgrass). Make sure the sparks don't fly onto clothing, and don't hold the smudge stick too close to someone's skin. Also be considerate enough to ask if people have allergies before you light incense.

Moon and Sun Water

Moon water is water that has been charged under the moon's energy. Sun water is water that has been charged by the light of the sun.

Full Moon Water

Fill a glass jar with water. Add a moonstone to the jar, and cap it. During the three nights of the full moon (the night before, the night of, and the night after) set the jar outside where it can capture the moon's rays (it doesn't matter if it is overcast). Bring the jar in each morning. After this, add water each month as needed, and set the jar outside the night before the full moon.

New Moon Water

Fill a glass jar with water. Add a piece of black onyx to the jar, and cap it. Follow the directions as above, but set the jar outside during the three nights of the new moon, instead of during the full moon.

Sun Water

Fill a glass jar with water. Add a piece of citrine or carnelian to the jar, and cap it. Set the jar outside on three consecutive sunny days, taking the jar inside at dusk. For added strength, set the jar outside at dawn on the morning of the summer solstice. Use sun water for solar rituals and spells.

Chakra Chart

CORRESPONDING COLORS FOR CHAKRAS

First Chakra (Base Chakra): Red

Second Chakra (Sacral Chakra): Orange

Third Chakra (Solar Plexus Chakra):
Yellow

Fourth Chakra (Heart Chakra): Green

Fifth Chakra (Throat Chakra): Blue

Sixth Chakra (Third Eye Chakra):
Indigo/Violet

Seventh Chakra (Crown Chakra):
White/Clear

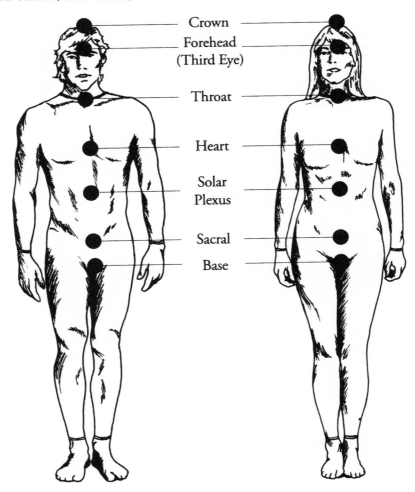

Crown

Forehead
(Third Eye)

Throat

Heart

Solar
Plexus

Sacral

Base

Resources

Suggested Music for Rituals and Meditations

* Corvus Corax

* Dead Can Dance

* Gabrielle Roth & The Mirrors

* Mike Oldfield

* Phil Thornton and Hossam Ramzy

* Suvarna

Suggested Reading

See the bibliography for reading recommendations.

Online Sites

Online sites come and go. If you do not find a site that is listed here, don't contact me about it. You might try a search on the name to see whether it has moved to a new URL.

General Magic

Circle Sanctuary: www.circlesanctuary.org

Galenorn En/Visions: www.galenorn.com

Gothic Gardening: www.gothic.net/~malice

JBL Statues: www.sacredsource.com

Mystickal Grove, A: www.amysticalgrove.com

New Moon Rising: www.nmrising.com (see also: Magical Magazines)

Nine Houses of Gaia, The: www.9houses.org

Pagans.org: www.pagans.org

Ravens World: www.ravensworld.com

Sakti Dances: www.witch.drak.net/moonsoul

Temple of Bastet: www.home.earthlink.net/~roscoecat

Wiccan-Pagan Times, The: www.twpt.com

Widdershins: www.widdershins.org (see also: Magical Magazines)

Witches' Voice, The: www.witchvox.com

Witch's Brew: www.witchs-brew.com

Dance

Art of Middle Eastern Dance, The: www.shira.net

Chainmail and More: www.sblades.com

Tribal Where?: www.tribalwhere.com

Magical Supplies

Most of the shops listed here offer mail-order and/or online service and catalogs. However, retail shops go in and out of business with alarming frequency, and web-based businesses can have an even briefer existence. So some of those shops listed may not be in service when you write to them.

As for as local supplies, look for candles in drug stores, stationery stores, grocery stores, and gift shops. Grocery stores and florists carry flowers, as do your friends' gardens. You can sometimes find essential oils in gift shops or perfume shops, and gift shops and rock shops may carry crystals. Gather your herbs wild or purchase them in grocery stores, food co-ops, herb shops, or local plant nurseries (the plant itself).

Unusual altar pieces can often be found at local import stores and secondhand stores. Altar cloths are easy; go to your favorite fabric shop and buy a piece of cloth large enough to cover your altar table.

Don't overlook the Yellow Pages. Look under Metaphysical, Herbs, Books (bookstores often carry much more than just books), Lapidary Supplies, and Jewelry.

Stores

Azure Green
48 Chester Road
Chester, MA 01011-9735
www.azuregreen.com

Eden Within
P.O. Box 667
Jamestown, NY 14702

Edge of the Circle Books
701 E. Pike
Seattle, WA 98122
(206) 726-1999

Gypsy Heaven
115 S. Main Street
New Hope, PA 18938
(catalog costs $3; refundable through money-order purchases only)

JBL Statues
Sacred Source / JBL
P.O. Box WW
Crozet, VA 22932-0163
Phone: (800) 290-6203
Phone: (804) 823-1515
Fax: (804) 823-7665
Email: spirit@sacredsource.com
www.sacredsource.com/

MoonScents and Magickal Blends
P.O. Box 3811588-LL
Cambridge, MA 02238

Serpentine Music Productions
P.O. Box 2564-L1
Sebastopol, CA 95473
(carries a wide variety of hard-to-find Pagan music)

White Light Pentacles
P.O. Box 8163
Salem, MA 01971-8163

Magical Magazines

Beltane Papers, The
P.O. Box 29694
Bellingham WA 98228-1694

New Moon Rising
P.O. Box 1731
Medford, OR 97501-0135
Phone: (541) 858-9404
Fax: (541) 779-8815
www.nmrising.com

Open Ways
P.O. Box 14415
Portland, OR 97293-0415

SageWoman
P.O. Box 641LL
Point Arena, CA 95648

Shaman's Drum
P.O. Box 430
Willits, CA 95490-0430

Widdershins
Emerald City/Silver Moon Productions
12345 Lake City Way NE, Suite 268
Seattle, WA 98125
www.widdershins.org

Glossary

Amulet. A magical charm.

Athame. A double-edged dagger used during ritual.

Aura. The energy field that surrounds all living things.

Censer. An incense burner.

Centering, to Center. The act of finding an internal point of balance and wholeness.

Chalice. A ritual goblet.

Charge. The act of energizing an object or person.

Circle. A sphere of energy, usually created by a Witch. It is considered to be sacred space.

Cleanse. The act of removing negative energy and purifying.

Craft. Witchcraft, the practice of natural magic.

Deosil. A clockwise (sunwise) direction.

Devocation. A formal farewell in ritual, usually to the gods and goddesses and/or elements.

Divination. The magical arts of discovering the hidden or the unknown through use of cards, runes, stones, crystals balls, and so on.

Dragon. A generic term for one of many mythological beasts that are reptilian in form; some are winged though most Oriental varieties are not; most dragons love treasure and are known to be exceptionally ancient and powerful spirits.

Dreamtime. The mystical void of creation, through which change can be effected upon the physical world.

Elements. The four building blocks of the universe—Earth, Air, Fire, and Water. These major forces are used in natural magic.

Evocation. A call to the spirits or other nonphysical entities.

Faerie. One of many nature spirits that inhabit a separate realm or dimension.

Faerie Kingdom. The realm of the Faerie.

Fetish. An amulet or talisman created to house the spirit of an animal totem or guide or to form a link with an animal spirit.

Fey. A being who is like or of the Faerie.

Futhark. The Norse rune alphabet.

Ground. The act of rooting oneself firmly in the physical world in preparation for magical or metaphysical work.

Hunt. The Wild Hunt led by (various) gods and/or goddesses.

Hunter. The Horned God of the Witches.

Invoke, Invocation. An appeal or petition to a god or goddess, an element, or an energy.

Ki-lin. The Chinese version of a unicorn.

Kirin. The Japanese version of a unicorn.

Magic, Magick. The manipulation of natural forces and psychic energy to bring about desired changes. Also referred to as magick by many Pagans.

Meditation. A state of reflection and/or contemplation.

Ogham. The Celtic rune alphabet.

Otherworld. Astral planes, where many mythological beasts make their home.

Pagan. A follower of Paganism.

Paganism. One of many ancient (and/or modern revivals of) Earth-centric and eco-centric religions.

Pentacle. A ritual object or piece of jewelry with a pentagram inscribed or woven into it.

Pentagram. A five-pointed star.

Phoenix. The Egyptian bird that was consumed by fire every five hundred years and rose, renewed, from the ashes.

Poppet. A figurine made of cloth, clay, wax, or wood that is used in magic to represent a specific person.

Reincarnation. The doctrine of rebirth. Most Pagans and Witches accept this as fact and see it as a part of the Wheel of Life.

Ritual. A ceremony.

Ritualist. One who takes part in a ritual.

Runes. Symbols that are carved onto rocks, crystals, or clay, which embody powerful energies to be used during magical practices. They are also symbols used in early alphabets.

Sabbat. One of the eight major Pagan holidays.

Samhain. A Sabbat festival celebrated every November 1 to honor and remember ancestors and the dead.

Scry. The act of gazing into or at an object while in trance, to open oneself to visions from the future or to discern hidden motives and energies behind an event or situation.

Shaman. A man or woman who has attained a high degree of knowledge concerning altered states of consciousness. Usually an honored title associated with a structured form of study in what are generally regarded as primitive or aboriginal religions.

Shamanism. The magical practice of shamans.

Spell. A magical ritual used to produce certain results in the physical world.

Talisman. A magically charged object used to attract a specific force or energy to its bearer.

Thunderbird. A Native American winged spirit, sometimes thought to be a great bird that can carry off human children or small animals; it wields the power of lightning.

Totem. An animal, plant, or mineral with which humans can form a soul connection.

Tradition. A specific subgroup of Pagans, Witches, Wiccans, or other magic workers.

Underworld. The realm of the spirit; the realm of the dead.

Unicorn. A magical horned horse.

Visualization. The process of forming mental images.

Wheel of Life. The cycle of birth, life, death, and then rebirth in a reincarnational sense.

Widdershins. A counterclockwise direction.

Witch. A practitioner of the craft of magic, or Witchcraft, usually also a member of a Pagan religion.

Witchcraft. The art of magic.

Bibliography

Books

Andrews, Ted. *Animal Speak*. St. Paul, MN: Llewellyn Worldwide, 1993.

———. *The Animal Wise Tarot*. Jackson, TN: Dragonhawk Publishing, 1999.

Biedermann, Hans. *The Dictionary of Symbolism*. New York, NY: Meridian, 1994.

Carr-Gomm, Philip and Stephanie. *The Druid Animal Oracle*. New York, NY: Fireside/Simon and Schuster, Inc., 1994.

Conway, D. J. *The Ancient and Shining Ones*. St. Paul, MN: Llewellyn Worldwide, 1993.

———. *Celtic Shamanism*. Freedom, CA: The Crossing Press, 2000.

Cunningham, Scott. *Encyclopedia of Magical Herbs*. St. Paul, MN: Llewellyn Worldwide, 1986.

———. *The Complete Book of Incense, Oils, and Brews*. St. Paul, MN: Llewellyn Worldwide, 1989.

Farrar, Janet and Stewart. *The Witches' Goddess*. Custer, WA: Phoenix Publishing Inc, 1987.

———. *The Witches' God*. Custer, WA: Phoenix Publishing Inc, 1989.

Galenorn, Yasmine. *Trancing the Witch's Wheel.* St. Paul, MN: Llewellyn Worldwide, 1997.

———. *Embracing the Moon.* St. Paul, MN: Llewellyn Worldwide, 1998.

———. *Dancing with the Sun.* St. Paul, MN: Llewellyn Worldwide, 1999.

———. *Magical Meditations.* Berkeley, CA: The Crossing Press, 2003.

Sams, Jamie. *Medicine Cards: The Discovery of Power through the Ways of Animals.* Santa Fe, NM: Bear and Company, 1988.

Sarangerel. *Riding Windhorses.* Rochester, VT: Destiny Books, 2000.

Sargent, Denny. *Global Ritualism.* St. Paul, MN: Llewellyn Worldwide, 1994.

Wolfe, Amber. *In The Shadow of the Shaman.* St. Paul, MN: Llewellyn Worldwide, 1990.

Online Resources

Totems, Shamanism, and Animals

* Animal Symbolism in Celtic Mythology: www-personal.umich.edu/~lars/rel375.html

* Beast Without, The, The Beast Within: www.atheling.demon.co.uk/animal_spirits.htm

* Course in Mongolian Shamanism, A: www.geocities/RainForest/Vines/2146/mongolia/cms.htm

* Encyclopedia Britannica: www.britannica.com

* Great Northern Hotel Owl's Nest, The: www.members.activecom.net/~smiller/owl.htm

* Guardian Geckos: www.coffeetimes.com/geckos.htm

* North American Wolf Association: www.nawa.org

* Spiritual Network: www.spiritualnetwork.net

General Mythology

* Crystal Links:www.crystalinks.com

* Encyclopedia Mythica: www.pantheon.org/mythica

* Gareth Long's Encyclopedia of Monsters, Mythical Creatures and Fabulous Beasts: www.webhome.idirect.com/~donlong/monsters/monsters.htm

* MapHist (an email discussion group): www.maphist.nl/index.html

* Mythical Creatures of Japan: www.suite101.com/article/cfm/japan_retired/15517

* Mything Links: www.mythinglinks.org

* Mythography: www.loggia.com/myth/myth.html

* Norse Creation Myth, The: www.pitt.edu/~dash/creation.html

* Web Resources for Early Scandinavia and the Gylfaginning: www-learning.berkeley.edu/wciv/ugis55a/readings/scandinavia.html

Dragons

* Archivald's Lair: www.angelfire.com/az2/dragonpractice

* Chinese Dragons: www.q-net.net.au/~dazsal/dragonspage.html

* Chinese Dragons: www.sorrel.humboldt.edu/~geog309i/ideas/dragons/chin.html

* Dragons of the British Isles, The: www.wyrm.demon.co.uk/ukdracs.htm

* Here Be Dragons: www.draconian.com

* Historical Dragon Page, The: http://bestiarium.net/index-e.html

Index